The Vision

The True and Untold Story of the Women's Basketball Association

The Vision

The True and Untold Story of the Women's Basketball Association

by
Lightning Ned Mitchell
as told to Mary-Lane Kamberg

Second edition 2017
Copyright © 2017, 2016 by Lightning Ned Mitchell
All rights reserved
Manufactured in the United States of America

ISBN-13: 978-1533194916
ISBN-10: 1533194912

Also available in Kindle EBook

Book Design by Gordon Kessler
Cover photo courtesy of Laura Allen
Cover photo: Baba Marshall, Evette Ott, Lighting N Mitchell
Members of the Women's Basketball Association,
a professional basketball league.

Praise for *The Vision*

Lightning Mitchell's compelling book *The Vision* is the true story about the origin of the Women's Basketball Association. His book brings to light the struggle and perseverance of the young women who became the first professional basketball players. The Vision is the heartfelt story of betrayal and disappointment for the teams, their coaches and their fans. In the blink of an eye a Vision can be lost to a more powerful entity which cannot be controlled. Lightning shares his God given plan to start the first ever women's professional spring/summer league. His book is an inspiration and a legacy to all the women's professional basketball players in the country. This book should be read by all.

—*Coach Marcus D. Harvey, head coach, player, teacher, and administrator, Penn Valley Community College*

...

With all the opportunities that have been denied women including going into the professional sports, I thought that the Women's Basketball Association would be something that Kansas City would be proud of for years and years to come. Today here's a story told about what took place, and it was here in Kansas City.

—*Congressman Emanuel Cleaver, II (D-Missouri), Former mayor of Kansas City, Missouri.*

In memory of Ollie Mae Mitchell, Ned Mitchell, and Billy Mitchell, and for all the girls and women who ever dreamed of playing professional basketball in the United States and for all the "little" people like me who refused to give up on a dream that God gave us. And most of all for the pioneering efforts of all the players, coaches, and staff who were part of the Women's Basketball Association.

—Lightning Mitchell.

For Coach Steve Ingram, Johanna Kamberg Falls, and the Olathe Tigers, Kansas Miracles, Kansas Thunderbolts, and Olathe South Lady Falcons.

—Mary-Lane Kamberg

"Not only is there more to life than basketball, there's a lot more to basketball than basketball."
—Phil Jackson

Table of Contents

Introduction 1
Chapter 1   In the Backcourt 3
Chapter 2   Tip-off 13
Chapter 3   Picks 21
Chapter 4   Road Games 31
Chapter 5   Full Court Press 51
Chapter 6   Benched 71
Chapter 7   Motion 81
Chapter 8   Fast Break 95
1995 WBA Rosters 106
Chapter 9   Air Ball 125
Chapter 10   Overtime 131
Chapter 11   Postgame 139
Women's Blue-Chip Basketball League, LLC 151
WBA Timeline 159
Photos of WBA Players and Teams 163
Newspaper Articles 171
Resources for Girls' and Women's Basketball 178
Assists (Acknowledgments) 181
My Prayer 183
Index 185
About the Authors 193

Introduction

In 1972 President Richard Nixon signed the federal Education Amendments of 1972, which included a provision commonly known as "Title IX," which had been introduced by Senator Birch Bayh of Indiana. The new amendments to the Higher Education Act prohibited discrimination based on gender in elementary and secondary schools, as well as colleges and universities, in all programs and activities – including sports. Until then women's athletic opportunities barely existed. Afterward, institutions of higher education offered varsity sports – with scholarships – to women, giving them a chance to improve their skills and continue to seek their full potential as athletes.

It took until 1976 for the Summer Olympics to add women's basketball for the first time. Meanwhile, elite female college players had nowhere in the United States to play after graduation. However, they found professional teams outside the country. In 1990 USA Basketball estimated that five hundred American women were playing basketball for teams in Asia,

Europe, Scandinavia, and South America. Two years later, an estimated eighty-five American women were playing with premier leagues in France, Italy, Spain, and Japan. Clearly there were female athletes who wanted to continue to play the game.

Twenty years after the signing of Title IX, and with God's help, I founded the Women's World Basketball Association, a name that was shortened to the Women's Basketball Association at the beginning of its inaugural season in 1993. I had played minor league professional football and was trying to return to professional sports, when God showed me a vision of a professional basketball league for women. At first I was reluctant to proceed. But whenever an obstacle presented itself, God saw to it that we overcame it.

The WWBA played an eleven-state exhibition tour in 1992, with a name change, new uniforms, and logos, followed by three fifteen-game spring-summer seasons from 1993-1995. The WBA was the first professional basketball league for men or women to play a summer season. The league had top quality players, who played hard buzzer-to-buzzer in every game. We proved that female athletes could be as exciting to watch as males. And we were selling franchises and building attendance numbers until the vision came to a sudden halt. **But this is why we're telling the story ... because we want to give credit where credit is due to the women in the WBA.**

— Lightning Ned Mitchell

Chapter 1
In the Backcourt

I sat in my living room in Independence, Missouri, in the spring of 1996 thinking about the upcoming season of the Women's Basketball Association (WBA) that I had founded four years earlier, when my brother Joe Lee Mitchell handed me a copy of the day's Kansas City *Star*.

I started to read. Right away one story caught my eye. Then I went numb the way you do when you learn of a death in the family. I stared at the newspaper but couldn't focus. I dropped the paper, slumped, and bowed my head.

"What is it?" Joe Lee asked.

"The NBA is starting a women's pro basketball league." I shook my head. "Those guys are giants. We can't compete with them."

I knew right away the news signaled the end to the WBA. I felt like a basketball player in a championship game whose team has led the whole way only to be beaten by an opponent's jump shot at the buzzer. That hopeless, empty feeling you get when you know there's nothing more you can do. That it's over.

I had founded the WBA as the Women's World Basketball Association (WWBA) to give American women a chance to play professional basketball here in the United States instead of having to play the professional game in other countries. But starting the league wasn't my idea. In fact, it was the furthest thing from my mind.

The idea was God's. And at the time I wasn't so sure it was a good one.

But I was sure that God wanted me to do it.

...

In fact, the sport of basketball itself was the furthest thing from my mind. Ever since high school I'd been intrigued with girls' basketball. I wasn't a huge fan, but I was interested. Back then girls' teams had six players each: three on the offensive and three on the defensive half of the court. A defensive player on one side of the court had to stop at the half-court line and pass the ball to a team-mate on the other side. I always wondered, why make them stop? I didn't go to a lot of girls' games, but I stayed interested.

But football was my game. I had played running back and outside linebacker on my Jackson High School football team in Jonesboro, Louisiana, and I was fast. Everyone thought I'd go to Grambling State University, a predominantly black college in Grambling, Louisiana, that was known for its football program. After that, I hoped to go to the National Football League.

But God had other plans. I graduated from high

The Vision

school in 1968 and got drafted – not by the NFL, but by the U.S. Army. I deployed to Viet Nam in 1969. Upon return to the United States, I played some college football. I was just a little older than most of the players, but I was still fast. That's when I got my new name. A bunch of fellow players were trying to come up with a nickname for me. There was a thunderstorm outside, and one of the guys got the idea. "Let's call him Lightning," he said. "Because he moves just like lightning. He's never in one spot too long."

I liked the nickname and later had my name legally changed to Lightning Mitchell.

After playing some college ball, I tried out for the Philadelphia Eagles NFL team and made the first cut for spring training with the rookies and the first-round through the last-round draft players. I made the first cut through that tryout and was invited back to the veteran's camp.

On the plane home from the tryouts, a fellow passenger recognized me from a photo and write-up in the sports pages. I was excited to be invited back. But for some reason I still can't explain to this day, I never returned to Philadelphia.

Since then I kept trying to think of ways to get back into the professional game. I thought I could get another shot at the NFL. I prayed a lot about it.

...

I played minor league football in Iowa for the Cedar Rapids Falcons, a farm team for the NFL's Atlanta Falcons. While there, I got a summer job through

Kirkwood Community College to supplement the money I was earning from football. The school had a lunch program for older citizens at several sites within about fifteen miles of each other. I worked at the Cedar Rapids Senior Citizen Community Center. Everyday, Monday through Friday, participants got together to eat lunch. The trouble was they just went home afterward. My task was to find something physical for them to do.

"Anything at all," my supervisor told me. "The guy who had the job before you got them to dance the polka."

I wondered what I could have these people do. Then I saw some seniors pushing something around on the floor. The site had a shuffleboard court, but my supervisor had told me, "They won't even pick up the sticks any more."

One day, I was out there just messing around. I showed a couple of women how to play shuffleboard, and some others wanted to learn, too. I got them comfortable with it at my site, and they began to enjoy it. Soon both men and women would just play around and practice after lunch. That's when I got the idea.

"I might be able to set up a shuffleboard league," I told them. "Would you want to do something like that?"

"Yeah," they said. "Yeah!"

Management gave me the go-ahead to start a league, but I would have to paint the shuffleboard courts myself. I went to six or eight different sites and told people at each site that I was going to start a league. They were excited about it. I put in the courts and made

The Vision

up schedules. Then people at all the sites wanted to play shuffleboard.

After lunch the seniors tried a few slides before the big game at 1 p.m. It got so bad, people wouldn't go home. After the game, they stayed to practice; they all wanted to be the best team. It got real serious, and the competition became stiff. It became a really big thing. Of course, then they had to have a tournament. I got sponsors for trophies and arranged for publicity. The local television station got hold of it and aired a story on the six o'clock news. They called it the Super Bowl Shuffleboard Tournament.

...

After six months, my job ended, and I moved to Janesville, Wisconsin, and played in a Triple-A professional football league in Delavan, Wisconsin. The league was similar to the minor leagues in baseball. Some players went from there to the ranks of the NFL. I wanted to get seen, and I was trying to get film footage to show I could still play. In the first game I got three carries for one hundred and five yards and a touchdown. I thought the NFL scouts would see my potential.

While living in Janesville I volunteered at the Salvation Army. I directed ongoing leagues for pool, table tennis, volleyball, and basketball for young and old, males and females. I enjoyed finding things for kids to do instead of just hanging around on the streets. I even got involved in finding sponsorships to fund the leagues. Two of my main sponsors were the American

Car Wash and James Fitzgerald, president of the National Basketball Association's Milwaukee Bucks.

It was 1991, and I was supplementing my football income by working at Sun Electric, a company that manufactured auto parts in Crystal Lake, Illinois, about an hour and a half commute from Delavan. My work station was the machine that stamped out parts for the Sun Electric Engine Distributor Diagnostics Tester, Model PDT-5D. The parts ran down a conveyer belt into a large basket on wheels.

I'd been praying, asking for God's guidance. What should I do with my life? One day I was alone in the room among humming machinery. I was thinking hard about my future and prayed again. I usually prayed, "Lord, help me get back into professional football." This time the wording was a little different. "Lord," I said, "please show me a way to get back into professional sports."

Now, I clearly meant back to the NFL. And even though I didn't say it this time, I'm sure God knew what I meant. But I asked to get back into "pro sports," and I hoped God would show me a way. When he did, I doubted what I heard. The voice was soft in my heart, but clear.

"Start a women's professional basketball league."

That was decidedly not what I had in mind. I looked to see where the voice came from, but no one else was around. It must have been noise from the machinery, I thought. But I heard it again. Again I ignored it. Maybe I needed more sleep. The third time, though, I knew the

The Vision

voice came from the Lord.

Still, I had my doubts about the message. The answer was nothing at all like what I had in mind. I was thinking I could return to professional sports as a player. I told myself I'd mention the idea of a women's league to my co-workers as we carpooled home. I thought, if they laugh, I'll laugh along with them and say I was just joking. If they think it's a bad idea, I'll leave it alone. I'll just put the idea out there.

After work I climbed into my black 626 Mazda four-door sedan. As usual, my coworker Mike Wilson and my brother Willie Mitchell rode home with me. I settled into the driver's seat and turned around. "What do you guys think about the idea of me starting a women's professional basketball league?"

To my surprise, neither laughed.

"Hmmm. That may be a good idea," Willie said. "There's not one anywhere."

Mike nodded.

That's when I knew it was time to pursue God's idea. OK, I thought, I'll do this, but I don't know how. God will have to help me.

...

At the time I didn't realize it, but God had already prepared me for this mission. Besides my experience with the Cedar Rapids shuffleboard tournament and the Salvation Army leagues in Wisconsin, I'd started a football league as a kid. Well, an electronic football league. When I was around the age of twelve, I had an electronic football game that I liked to play, and I went around and showed it to the other kids. "Ask your parents to get you one of these."

They did, and I set up a league and a schedule. Everyone played each other, and we ended with a championship game. I also set up a one-on-one basketball league for my friends. I organized all the games for everybody. But God wasn't through preparing me for this crazy idea of starting a women's professional basketball league.

...

Even as a kid I was always interested in the Word of God. My grandfather was a preacher, and I thought it would be neat to do that. By the time I was around ten or twelve, I took my interest to another stage.

I liked to catch butterflies, bumble bees, and grasshoppers in Ball brand canning jars with silver tops. I built three cages – one for each species – and put them out on our porch. The cages had three wooden sides and a top and bottom, all about a foot square. I used screening for the fourth side so the bugs would have a window to look out. I also made a little door in the back that I could open and close to put the bugs in there. I gave them flowers to eat.

One day I decided I needed to do more and decided to sing to them. I sang gospel songs. Then I started preaching to them. They became my congregation. When my mom's friends were over visiting, I'd go out to the porch.

"He's getting ready to hold services with his insects," Mom told her friends.

The Vision

Looking back, I think it's strange that I did stuff like that, but I think that's about the time people started calling me Preacher. They'd see me walking and say things like, "There goes Preacher."

People kept telling me, "You gonna be a preacher just like your grandfather."

Later on in life, though, I thought if I were going to be a preacher, God would equip me for it. I didn't want to go to a seminary to learn Man's philosophy. I would come to it the way Moses, Abraham, Isaac, and David came to it. I wanted to be like them. If God wanted me to be a preacher, God would give me everything I needed and prepare me with his Word.

...

During high school I really believed that God had his hand on my life in some kind of way. And I had a strong example. Once all the boys decided to go swimming at a nearby fishing pond. I went along even though I didn't know how to swim. They were all jumping in and swimming around, and I was on the shore. There was a boat floating out on the pond.

As I watched my friends moving their arms and kicking, I thought I'd try to do what they were doing. I got in the water and tried it, but I went under.

I surfaced and yelled, "Help! Help!"

I was flailing around and went under again. Suddenly, I found myself in the boat. I looked around. "Who helped me into the boat?"

My friends looked at each other. "What do you mean? We thought you got into the boat on the shore."

I shook my head. "No, it was already out here on the water."

They shrugged.

I have no idea how I got into that boat, but I know someone helped me. And it sure wasn't any of my friends.

Chapter 2
Tip-off

As I went about taking steps to fulfill the vision of a women's professional basketball league, God was always there making things happen; I just wasn't acknowledging it yet. Soon, though, I would make the connection. Everything I needed was "just there."

"Everything" included a place for tryouts, players' jerseys, and even team vans to take to games. In fact, for every question I had, God had an answer. Every need was provided for. Every problem was solved. I began to realize that as long as I was willing to be used as an instrument in God's hand, God would provide everything necessary to accomplish His task.

My first step was coming up with a name for the league. I was thinking "NBA-WBA," like that. I ended up choosing the Women's World Basketball Association. I needed a place to work, but I lived alone then. I decided to work out of my home.

Next, I needed players. And I needed to make it known to the public and the world that this was happening. To get a feel for the level of interest out there, my assistant Vickie Schmidt wrote a letter to send to women's college basketball coaches explaining who I was and the purpose of the league – to give women the chance to play professional basketball in the United States without having to go overseas to do it. I asked for the coaches' assistance in inviting any graduating seniors who were interested. I enclosed a form for them to sign their names and addresses and return to me.

Early in 1992 I contacted the National Collegiate Athletics Association headquarters in Overland Park, Kansas, (they since moved to Indianapolis, Indiana) and got a list of all the NCAA women's basketball programs at Division I, II, and III colleges and universities. I sent the letter to one hundred thirty-six schools. I didn't limit the recruiting to Division I schools, because I knew Division II and Division III schools also had talented athletes who should have a shot at playing.

Many of the coaches were very supportive. Pat Summitt, the legendary women's basketball coach from the University of Tennessee, Marian Washington from the University of Kansas, and Vivian Stringer from the University of Iowa (and later, Rutgers University) offered helpful insight. So did Leon Barmore, head coach of the Lady Techsters at Louisiana Tech University; Lynnette Woodard, the first female member of the Harlem Globetrotters; and Nancy "Lady Magic" Lieberman, the first woman to coach a professional men's team – the Texas Legends in the NBA's development league.

Despite their help, players' response to my letters was not as great as I expected. I probably got maybe twelve or thirteen forms back. I was getting nervous, but I had to move forward. I decided to take two teams on an exhibition tour to gauge interest in women's professional basketball before embarking on a full-fledged league.

...

My plan for the tour included Midwestern cities in a close range. We wouldn't have money to fly anywhere. We'd be driving vans. I decided the tour would leave from Kansas City, Missouri, and we'd play our first game in St. Joseph, Missouri, north of the city.

The original plan called for games in Greeley, Colorado; Fargo, North Dakota (a nice area for girls and women's basketball); Des Moines, Iowa; Gary, Indiana; Chicago, Illinois; St. Paul, Minnesota (another area where girls and women's basketball was strong); then back to play in Kansas City, Kansas, and Kansas City, Missouri. From there we'd go to Beatrice, Nebraska (near Omaha), and then on to Miami, Oklahoma.

...

As I was making these preparations, a nagging doubt crept into my mind. I was still a little unsure about this venture. It was like the story of Moses and the splitting of the Red Sea. God had led the people through and onto dry land, but they still had the audacity to question whether Moses should be leading them or not and whining about lack of water and food in the desert. Apparently, the miracle of the sea wasn't sufficient. My lack of faith was like that of those people. Despite what God had already shown me, I still doubted Him. I tested him by asking for more signs.

One night after work, I rode home alone. Mike and Willie usually rode home with me, but this night they had come in early and left before me. On the way home I thought about the basketball idea. I said, "Lord, if this is something you want me to do, could you give me some type of sign?"

I looked up and saw a falling star. Was that my sign? I'd seen falling stars before. It wasn't that unusual. But before doubt settled in my brain, I saw three or four more stars falling right behind one another in rapid fire. That was out of the ordinary. That was my sign.

For the tryout venue, my first thought was to use the YMCA in Janesville, Wisconsin. They had a beautiful facility with a nice gym. I lifted weights there three times a week, and I knew the director. I also coached a YMCA youth football team and a girls' basketball team there, so the kids that no other coaches wanted would have a chance to play. But as I pursued the Y, I had a heavy feeling that it wasn't right. I was fighting that feeling. I knew I couldn't afford anything else. And I was friends with the head of the Y. I knew I could get it for the tryouts.

I kept sensing God nudging me to get the training center in St. Francis, Wisconsin, used by the Milwaukee Bucks NBA team. I was sure Cousins Center would cost thousands of dollars, and I knew I couldn't afford it. But

The Vision

I couldn't get rid of the uneasy feeling. I decided at least to make an attempt to get it to prove to God that I couldn't afford it. I would call and get the amount. Once that was done, I'd go back to the Y. I had it set in my mind that that's where I'd hold the tryouts, and I wasn't going to change my mind.

I phoned the Bucks in May and told them my intent. "Do you rent out your training facility?" I was sure the woman I talked to would say no.

"Yes, all the time," she said, "as long as it doesn't interfere with something we're doing. What dates are you interested in?"

"July 24, 25, and 26."

"Oh, I'm sorry. That's our rookie tryout camp. Are there any other dates you can use?"

"No, it has to be those dates." I wanted to start the exhibition tour in August so the season could start the following April after March Madness. I didn't want to compete with the traditional men's basketball season. And I didn't want to compete with football.

Plus, I wanted to show God that the Y was the best place for the tryouts. I was happy! Now I could give up and go back to the Y. I was ready to hang up when the woman stopped me.

"Wait a minute," she said. "Let me check something."

I waited.

She came back on the phone. "You can have those dates. This year we moved the tryouts to Denver."

That was OK so far, but cost was the real barrier.

"How do you want it set up?" she asked. "Do you want it like we set up for the Bucks with the bleachers and everything?"

I figured that would cost extra. And I wanted to run up the cost, so I could be right about not being able to afford it. "Yes."

"Hot or cold showers?"

"Which is more expensive?"

"Hot."

"Hot then." The whir of a calculator sounded in the background.

"Towels?"

"Do they cost extra?"

"A little."

"Give 'em to me." More sounds came from the calculator.

"Water or Gatorade?"

"Definitely Gatorade."

"Do you want referees?"

"Yes."

"Do you want us to contact the media or do you want to do it?

Everything she could come up with, I said, "Give it to me."

"Is that it?" she asked.

"I think you got it all."

The calculator kept whirring. I'm happy. I'm thinking this will cost about fifteen thousand dollars. The calculator stopped.

"Are you ready for this?" she asked.

18

The Vision

"Yes. Let me sit down."

"That will be one-seventy-six, twelve."

"One-hundred and seventy-six thousand?"

"No. Dollars. One-hundred and seventy-six dollars. And twelve cents."

I sat in stunned silence. I could not believe it! I had two hundred dollars cash in my pocket! I booked the dates. From that moment I went from disbelieving to deciding that I should never give up on anything I was trying to do.

...

With the tryout site decided, I called coaches at schools close to the tryout site. I spoke to Ann Smith and Bob Hawkins, who agreed to host the tryouts and choose the players for me.

As the tryout date got closer, I only had one or two more letters from prospective players. The arena was ready. The media had already been contacted. I was getting scared. But I pushed forward. I sent news releases asking for players to newspapers in nearby Milwaukee, Janesville, and Madison and hoped for the best.

...

I realized I needed some type of jerseys for the athletes to wear for the tryouts. I'd become good friends with Tom Burer from shopping at Saxer's Sporting Goods, the biggest sporting goods store in Janesville. Tom's father-in-law, John Saxer, owned the store. I contacted Tom and told him what I was trying to do.

"I need some stuff," I said. "Can you help me?"

"What do you need?"

"Basketball jerseys."

"How many?"

"At least twenty-two," I said. "Eleven for each team. And I'm going to need some basketballs."

Tom and I had been friends for many years. He had done a lot of things for me out of the kindness of his heart and had taken a great loss. But once again, without hesitation, he came through for me. He gave me everything I needed to host the tryouts. I would forever be indebted to him.

I had no problems.

Yet.

Chapter 3
Picks

The first day of tryouts I got up early. The tryouts were set for ten A.M. I dressed looking sharp in a white polo shirt with the league logo on the left side and my name on the right side. My mood was dampened by heavy fog and temperature in the sixties – in July! I hoped the dreary day wouldn't keep players away. I prayed for a decent turnout.

The Bucks training facility, a 35,000 square-foot wing of the Archbishop Cousins Center in St. Francis, Wisconsin, had a full-size professional 94-foot by 50-foot regulation basketball floor, with six additional baskets for shooting drills. The hunter green, silver, and purple team colors decorated the floor. The gym had a real professional feel to it, with bleachers and everything their regular arena had – even banners hanging on the walls. The Bucks' personnel had everything ready for us.

The media arrived first, followed by three prospective players. A guy from a local television station looked around and asked me, "Anybody going to show up?"

I spoke with confidence. "Oh yeah, they'll be here."

It was five minutes till ten. A couple more players arrived.

"Now he's got five!" another reporter in a blue striped tie shouted.

A newspaper reporter chimed in. "It will be embarrassing if no one shows up."

I went over to him, again with confidence. "They'll be here."

I had no idea if I'd have even ten people. My stomach was turning inside out. I was thinking how embarrassing it would be. I'm a stubborn man, and I had faith. But faith without works doesn't work. You have to do the work and trust the rest will come.

Had I done enough?

I went alone to a locker room to pray. I sat on a bench and bowed my head. My hope was gone, and I was extremely worried. "God, help me." I splashed water on my face, dried off, and went back out there.

When I got back to the court, the thump, thump, thump of bouncing basketballs greeted me. Players streamed in carrying duffle bags. The guys from the media were clapping. My spirits lifted. I took a deep breath and relaxed.

The reporters gathered around as I met with the athletes and told them what we were trying to accomplish. "The road won't be easy. We're going to be pioneers of women playing professional ball in the

The Vision

United States. You won't have to go overseas to play or settle for ending your careers with the college game any longer. I think the public is ready to accept women's professional sports, and you're going to show them why."

I paused and looked at the group. They were paying rapt attention. "We'll put in a lot of work now. We'll pay your expenses. We want to split revenues with you guys, but we have to cover the expenses of the next game before we can."

I introduced the coaches. "Ann Smith and Bob Hawkins are going to pick twenty-two of you to go on a twelve-week, eleven-state exhibition tour, so we can get an idea of the amount of fan interest out there. Then we'll see about starting a league next spring."

I gave them the basics. "We'll have a twenty-four-second shot clock and play strictly man-to-man, run-and-gun. We'll use NBA rules. We'll play twelve-minute quarters, and you get six fouls. We're not bending the rules or lowering the baskets."

I wanted a twenty-four second shot clock to speed up the game, increase the number of shots taken, and put more scores on the board. The thirty-second clock used in college gave too much time to set up plays. With the twenty-four second clock, you didn't have much time to set up a play by the time you got the ball to the other end of the court. We wanted lots of running and shooting. The WWBA and NBA players shot the same free throws, and the three-point line was the same.

I had heard that in the late 1970s the former

Women's Basketball League had encouraged their players to go to charm school and get training in wearing make-up. The players had resented it, and I wasn't going to make an exhibit out of young women to promote the league. Their basketball talent would be the main attraction.

The coaches took over, and more sounds of dribbling balls and shots hitting the glass filled the training center. The coaches had the girls stretch and run some drills. Then the players broke into groups and shot lay-ups, jump shots, and free throws. They played half-court three-on-three and rotated players. They played five-on-five, and the coaches substituted players in and out. At the end of the three days, we announced the list of players selected.

"If you're on the list, let us know when and where we'll meet to begin the tour," I said. "If you can't go, we'll replace you with another player. If you're not on the list, it doesn't mean you're not part of this. No one is cut. We'll contact you later. You'll be part of a franchise but not on the tour."

Everyone on the list wanted to go on the tour. The players chatted among themselves. The atmosphere was electric.

...

We divided them into an American Team and a National Team. The girls loved basketball and were devoted to our new league. They had been outstanding college athletes. And they had unbelievable talent. I was honored to have them.

The Vision

For instance, Diana Vines, a 5'11" guard/forward averaged 30 points per game and made 85 percent of her free-throws in her senior year at DePaul University in Chicago. She was named Most Valuable Player of the Women's National Invitational Tournament in 1988. As of 2016 she was still listed as the school's all-time leading scorer with 2,504 career points. She was also still listed as the all-time top free throw shooter, with 586 made shots, and in second as the all-time rebounder with an average of 10.5 boards per game.

Lisa Long starred at the University of Iowa from 1983 to 1987. She was named to the United States Select Team in 1986 and earned 1987 All-Big Ten honors as a senior. That year Iowa made it to the Elite Eight in the National Collegiate Athletics Association women's tournament.

In 1983 Priscilla Gary was Kansas State University's first Kodak All-America player. That year the Wildcats won all fourteen home games and reached the Sweet Sixteen in the NCAA tournament.

A 5-foot, 10-inch first-team Gateway Collegiate Athletic Conference forward from Eastern Illinois University, Chris Aldridge was known for her leaping ability. She could grab the rim. In 2012 she was still listed in the school's all-time Top Ten in field goals attempted, field goals made, free throws attempted, rebounds, and steals. Her career 1,337 points between 1982 and 1986 earned her a spot in the school's 1,000-Point Club.

Trish Williamson played at the University of

Northern Colorado from 1987 to 1991. She was the school's first first-team All-America women's basketball player as a senior. When she graduated she was the Bears' all-time leading scorer and rebounder. She was named to the North Central Conference All-Conference Teams in 1989 and 1991. In 1991 she ranked twelfth in the nation in scoring, averaging 21.9 points per game. She scored 30 points or more in five collegiate games. She was inducted into the University of Northern Colorado Hall of Fame in 2009.

Also from the University of Northern Colorado was Lisa Burch, who had the most steals (85) in the 1990-91 season, a record that held for decades.

At guard, Stephanie Worthy was an NAIA Second Team All-America in 1985 and a First Team All-America selection in 1986. She had an 18.9-point career scoring average at the University of Missouri-Kansas City (UMKC) and as of 2014 remained the school's top all-time career scorer. She was inducted into the UMKC Hall of Fame in 2008.

At 5-foot, 6-inch feisty point guard Geri "Kay Kay" Hart came from the University of Kansas. Lynn Page a 6-foot, 4-inch center also joined us from the Jayhawks.

Robelyn Annette "Robbie" Garcia was a great ball handler, passer, and scorer. The guard played collegiate basketball at Dodge City College and the University of Nebraska. At Dodge City she was a Region NJCAA All-America and led the nation in scoring as a freshman when she averaged 31.5 points per game *before* the game included a three-point line. In her two years there

The Vision

she scored 1,298 points and had two career-high games of 46 points and 40 points. She was ranked as one of the top junior college swing guards in the country. She played her senior year at Friends University, where she averaged 20 points per game and was a unanimous Kansas Collegiate Athletic Conference First-Team selection and an NAIA Region All-Star.

Pam Cox was an awesome ballplayer. She was a 1985-1986 All-America athlete at Western Texas College. I remember Pam as a leader who also tried to keep the players together. If a player was struggling, Pam always encouraged that player and built her up.

As a high school senior Melissa Sanford was named to the National High School Coaches All-America team. In her three-year career, she scored 894 points and had 425 assists, 197 steals, and 82 blocked shots. She played one year at the University of Nebraska then transferred to Creighton University in Omaha where she finished her college career. During those three years, she scored 1,173 career points and had a 40-percent three-point field goal average. She was a Michael Jordan in the WWBA. She could do everything with the ball but make it talk, and I think if she really wanted to she could have made it talk, too. She was a scorer, a team player, and a morale builder. She gave it all to win. She played for the WWBA's Nebraska Xpress. In a league play-off game against the Kansas Crusaders, she played with a broken nose that she got in a game two weeks prior.

Renee Dozier had played at the University of

Missouri-Columbia. In the 1994-1995 WBA season, she was the defensive player of the year and one of the league's best rebounders.

Lisa Carlsen, who had played at Northwest Missouri State University, became a special player to me. She was a four-time all-conference basketball honoree. In her senior year, Carlsen was named the 1992 Champion NCAA Female Athlete of the Year. She was selected for the tour, and continued to play in the league until it folded in 1996.

One of the girls who tried out was a high school basketball star in Casper, Wyoming. Sheryl Schroefel didn't get a Division I scholarship, but she played college ball in the Missouri Ozarks. I watched her in the tryouts. All I saw was hustle, hustle, hustle. She never quit, just like the Energizer bunny. You could see her love of the game.

...

After the tryout I was happy everything turned out so well, but I worried, too. I didn't yet have any arenas lined up. What would I do about transportation? And how was I going to get money for the tour?

I had quit my job at Sun Electric to focus on the league, and I wanted to move the league office to a better location – one located in a strong women's basketball atmosphere. Iowa was the nation's women's basketball capital, so I moved to Des Moines, home of Drake University. I tried to line up Drake's arena for one of the league's franchise sites, but that didn't work out. We scheduled one tour game there, but the arena

The Vision

was in high demand, and there were too many scheduling conflicts to play a whole season there.

I was running out of money, so I moved to Kansas City. My sister Linda Mae Bell lived there, and I moved in with her. I set up another home office and started working on the tour.

Soon after that, I married Brenda Warner, and she moved in with Linda and me. Brenda worked for a home building contractor and supported the two of us. While I worked on the league, we lived off her income. She also supported my efforts by sending out information and doing other clerical work for the league.

I continued to plan the tour. We would need places to stay, so I contacted the corporate offices for hotels in the cities we'd travel to. I followed up with a letter saying what we were doing and the type of promotion they'd get at the events. I also assured them that any parents or friends who came along with us would stay with them, too. The hotels agreed to free rooms or half-price discounts for the players' and coaches' rooms.

I had made hotel reservations for each stop, but I didn't have enough funds. I did have emergency back-up. Before we left, my brother Joe Lee Mitchell approached me. "Man, I know you're in some trouble," he said. He gave me his American Express credit card. "If you need to use it, use it."

I shook my head. "No. I don't want to put your family in jeopardy."

"Take it," he said. "Don't use it if you don't need it. But if you need it, use it."

Through corporate sponsorships we got the other things we needed. Russell Athletics provided uniforms, and Baden Basketballs gave us leather balls. I arranged transportation through System One Car Rental (which was later taken over by Enterprise Rent-A-Car). We struck a deal that we'd promote them at every stop along the tour. They gave me two new fifteen-passenger rental vans to use. The players knew what to expect. I'd told them we weren't flying anywhere in luxury airplanes, but we hoped that if the league caught on, that might be in their futures.

With all that in place, the Women's World Basketball Association All-star teams were ready to hit the road for their Bustin' Out Tour.

Chapter 4
Road Games

The players and coaches met me on the Monday before the first game at a Quik Trip parking lot off Interstate-435 in northeast Kansas City, Missouri, near the World's of Fun/Oceans of Fun theme parks. Larry Fields and Tiny Hovet would coach the teams. I had played football with Larry, who sported a bushy black mustache. We were both on the Cedar Rapids Falcons, Triple-A pro football team. Since then Larry had been coaching middle school basketball in Cedar Rapids for fifteen years.

Tiny had answered one of my ads. He was about 5-foot, 7-inches and about 160 pounds. He was a military guy and well disciplined in everything. Tiny had coached girls' high school basketball in Fargo, North Dakota. He also had some experience as an assistant coach at the college level. They both loved women's basketball and would have given up anything to be part of the new league.

As the players arrived at the Quik Trip, they

huddled together in small circles talking to each other in excited tones. This thing was really going to happen. The players piled into the shiny, white vans – one for the National team and one for the American team. My brother Willie, who had worked with me at Sun Electric and was in the carpool the night God told me to start the league, came along with his wife Alyce Mitchell. Willie would drive one van, and Larry and Tiny would trade off driving the other. I led the caravan in my used black Lincoln Continental. The car had more than 200,000 miles on it, and was on its last legs. The car made it all the way through the tour (thank God!) with no issues.

We drove out. I worried about being able to cover food and expenses, because I didn't have a million dollars in my pocket.

...

We arrived at the Ramada Inn in St. Joseph, and the manager honored our agreement to charge half-price for the rooms in exchange for advertising at the games. I told the manager at a nearby Kentucky Fried Chicken that we'd promote his location at the game, and he fed the girls for free.

But our first obstacle reared its head shortly after we arrived. For the first game, I had reserved the Civic Arena, a multi-use public facility that had opened in 1980. It had a portable 60-foot by 112-foot wooden basketball floor and permanent seating for 2,300 fans, with an option of 1,500 additional seating. However, I hadn't firmed up the price. I was thinking it would be a maximum of five hundred dollars. But when we got there I found out the price was fifteen hundred dollars! That was way outside our budget.

We had to scramble to secure a place to play.

Once again, God came through with a solution. Someone in St. Joseph knew that the Leavenworth High School girls' team had just come off three great seasons. In fact, two Leavenworth players had won the annual Kansas Basketball Coaches Association's Miss Kansas Basketball honors as the top girls' high school basketball players in the state: Nicole Coates in 1989 and Kelly Dougherty in 1990. The city of Leavenworth lies fewer than forty miles southwest of our St. Joseph hotel on the Kansas side of the Missouri River.

The area's interest in female basketball made the high school a nice option for our first game. I contacted school district officials, who agreed to let us use their facility for a discounted fee. We went to work promoting the tour. The WWBA players met the coach and players of Leavenworth High School basketball team, and the coach helped us promote the event. We handed out free tickets to the high school girls. (Of course, we knew that the girls wouldn't come alone, and we'd sell tickets to their parents!) Once we had the venue locked in, we contacted area newspapers and other media to spread the word that we were in town.

At game time we had 150 fans in gym. The fans were very supportive. I think they were surprised how well the women played. We used NCAA Division I referees for our games.

However, after the game, I was disappointed. Things didn't go as well as I expected in terms of turnout. I thought we'd open the doors and have six hundred people there. We'd lost a lot of money, and funds were already low. But, we packed the van and headed to Greeley, Colorado, for the next game. I drove by myself, worrying. I prayed, "Lord, I have twenty-two players and two coaches depending on me. I have to feed them and pay for hotel rooms." Of course, God already knew this anyway. I continued, "Lord, I know your plan, but I need a little help here."

In Greeley I didn't want anyone to know my negative thoughts. We needed to regroup. Despite my efforts to hide my feelings, some of the players thought something was going on with me. I think they could see I was struggling and wanted to help.

Two of them came to me. One said, "You need to let us help you do some stuff."

I shook my head. "You just need to play ball."

"We can go out and talk to people and give out tickets," the other one said.

"Good," I said. You do that, and I'll work on places to get people to give us meals." I felt good. God was sending me help. My players wanted to make this work.

Players from both teams joined Trish Williamson, who had played college ball at the University of Northern Colorado in Greeley, and held a basketball clinic for high school players at the Conditioning Spa. Brett Amole, a photographer from the Greeley *Tribune* showed up, and the paper ran a photo and a story promoting our upcoming game.

I found a restaurant willing to sponsor (and feed) us in exchange for promoting them during the game. That's where the idea of trading advertising at the game for goods and services came from. We used the same method for the rest of the tour.

Then we got more help from Greeley Mayor Willie Morton. He got behind us and set up some kind of scheme to get people to come. He said the city would give away something, but you had to be present to win. I was overwhelmed with the mayor's support. I thought this can really work. The raffle, however, was a big joke. Nobody had the correct ticket. And no prize was given away. The mayor didn't even show up for the game!

But fans did. People were interested in the idea of women's professional basketball. Two of our players had played college ball at the University of Northern Colorado, where we held the game at Butler-Hancock Hall. Trish Williamson played for the World Conference team, and Lisa Burch played for the American Conference team. Their UNC coach, Janet Schafer, attended the game.

Even though each team had only seven players (because of illness and college graduations), the players who were there put on a good show. Fans sat on the edge of their seats the whole time. Both teams came to play, but the American Conference team used an 18-4 run near the end of the first quarter to lead 37-14. By half time the score was 57-45.

"We came out psyched up and playing a lot of team

ball," Lisa Burch told the Greeley *Tribune*. "We were just really excited to play."

The Americans seemed to shoot one hundred percent, but I knew the World team would start hitting. And they did. The World team took the lead for the first time on a fast-break layup by Dawne Gittens during the third quarter. By the end of the period, they held the lead 77-76. The lead bounced back and forth during the last quarter. With about four minutes left, the Americans led 97-92. But Williamson was not to be denied. She scored three baskets in a row. Her World Conference team held on and won 106-103.

"I missed some shots that I should've made," Trish Williamson told the *Tribune*. "I just talked to myself, and they started going in."

In my book both teams were winners.

After the game Coach Schafer told the *Tribune,* "I think (the new league) is great, and I hope it goes far. Something like this is needed, and it's a good opportunity for Trish and Lisa to get involved."

Greeley was a real eye opener. I learned to trust in God, not my own feelings.

In the game, one of our players broke her ankle, and we took her to a hospital in Greeley. Doctors set the break, but she was unable to continue the tour. This girl was an All-America-type player. She could dribble the ball between her legs. She could do anything. She would have beaten the average guy. She sobbed. "I really wanted to play."

"Go home and get yourself ready for the season," I

The Vision

said.

She looked up. "You mean you're not going to cut me?

I scoffed. "Shut up!"

She smiled. "Don't worry, I'll be ready."

I called one of the stand-by players, who lived in Wisconsin. "Can you join the tour in a couple of weeks?"

I could almost hear her smile over the phone. "I didn't think you'd call me."

"We'll pick you up in St. Cloud, Minnesota, and take you on to the game in St. Paul."

"My parents will drive me there."

...

As the twelve-week tour rolled on, we followed the same pattern. We arrived in a new city on Monday and enjoyed discounts at our motels. Often, their signs welcomed the WWBA all-star players and told when and where we'd be playing.

We negotiated with local Kentucky Fried Chicken restaurants and such others as Baker's Square, Burger King, Denny's, Hardee's, and McDonald's. They bought into the same deal – they fed us in exchange for advertising at the event. So did several small mom-and-pop cafes and restaurants. We visited car dealerships and other businesses in the area. We offered free tickets to businesses that supported us, and we also offered to promote the businesses during the game.

Promotion of the exhibition games started when we arrived in each city. We went to the media to let them know we were there. I knew I had to promote the exhibition games, but I had no idea that I could do it. I'd never done it before. My only experience with public speaking had been preaching to my bees and butterflies on my mother's porch. But when the time came to do media interviews, I was up to the task.

The players became famous once we hit town. They wore their shirts with the logos on them and handed out flyers at retail stores. Car dealers ran radio ads saying the teams would appear at their stores to sign autographs. The players also signed autographs at the hotel and let kids take pictures with them.

During the week, the teams practiced two or three times at the court where they would play. In addition to Leavenworth High School in Kansas, three colleges and four city-owned auditoriums in other states let us use their arenas for free. I had never experienced such generosity so freely given. I began to see that if I let God use me as his instrument, He would provide everything necessary to accomplish His work. I also became aware of the way God worked through individuals to assist us.

Players sold tickets to local businesses. And we gave away free tickets to local players on girls' high school basketball teams, hoping that their parents would bring them and become paying customers. The promotion efforts helped. Kids who fell in love with the players at the autograph sessions came to the Saturday night games. On Sundays we drove to the next destination.

...

Team bonding began on the road. Over the twelve-

The Vision

week tour, the players became close. They were more than a team. They were a family. They cared about the cities that we played in, especially the kids, who always got special attention. Sometimes the players gave kids their own special belongings like a bracelet or picture or autographed T-shirt. All of the players on the tour did this. I can't single out a certain player who did this or that, because they all did things as a team. What one did, they all did. If one went to the movies they all went, if one got hungry they were all hungry, if one was hurting they were all hurting. And these girls always wanted to go to church on Sunday before we left each town.

I'd never before seen such a close bond among team-mates. It was the type of bond that we need here in the world today, the love that they had is unexplainable. Robbie Garcia, who was on the tour and later played for the Kansas Crusaders and the Kansas City Mustangs said, "The largest impact the WBA had on my personal life was providing the sense of belongingness I had always searched for as an adoptee. My teammates were my sisters. My coaches bestowed guidance, and the fans instilled acceptance!"

I don't know if it was because of the tour itself or being away from their families, but I really believe it was because of the bond God put around the whole tour.

...

After Greeley, whenever we went to a new city, we were like a circus coming to town. I always tried to get the mayor and Chamber of Commerce on our side.

Sports editors in the cities were supportive, and we got plenty of ink the week we were there. We contacted high school principals and our players visited girls' basketball teams and talked about the future.

"One day," they told the players, "you'll have the opportunity to play professional ball."

We had planned our next game after Greeley for Fargo, North Dakota. But I looked at the map. We were just down the road from Casper, Wyoming, where Sheryl Schroefel had played high school basketball. I thought it would be fun for her to play at home, and Greeley was close enough to Casper that I looked into going there. We planned everything at the last minute, and the Day's Inn gave us a big discount on lodging.

When Sheryl found out, she was so excited. She called her parents, who still lived there, to tell everybody we were coming. Her family started the promotion before we arrived. They did a lot of the footwork. The local newspaper couldn't wait for us to get there. In high school, Sheryl had been everybody's favorite, and our teams got the red carpet treatment. We had a great crowd, and the stop was the high point of the tour.

Sheryl played well during that game. She was go and go and go. This girl would not stop. She was a defensive nut. She was like a worry, and she got on the nerves of the players she was guarding. She was all in-your-face. If an opponent got angry, Sheryl would take the ball away from her. She was unbelievable.

...

We got another good reception the following week in

The Vision

Des Moines, Iowa. When we got situated at the hotel, the desk clerk handed me a note.

Call city hall.

I phoned and got the mayor's assistant.

"Are you guys in town?" he asked. "The mayor wants to meet with the girls tomorrow."

I never expected that. The next day the mayor welcomed us. The girls were wearing their uniforms. At the mayor's suggestion, they gathered around him for a photo to show support for the fledgling league. The picture ran in the Des Moines *Register*. It was great publicity for us.

We played at Drake University in Des Moines, Iowa, another hotbed of women's basketball at the time. This was an interesting game. We had players from Drake, Iowa State, and the University of Iowa. They brought in a lot of local fans who remembered them.

...

The next day we headed for Gary, Indiana. Somewhere along the way, I checked my rearview mirror. One of the vans was missing. I saw only my brother Willie Mitchell's.

I pulled over and flagged him down. "Where's the other van?"

"They're behind us," he said. He looked back down the road. "They were behind me!"

We had pagers back then, but no cell phones. And there was no such thing as GPS. Tiny Hovet couldn't let us know where he was. I left Willie on the side of the road and backtracked down the highway. Several miles later, I saw the other van. It was pulled over with lights flashing, out of gas.

"I'm sorry, Lightning," Tiny shook his head. "I thought I had enough gas when we left. Guess I was wrong."

The players didn't care. They were walking around outside the van having a good time. "We thought you wouldn't notice we weren't behind you until you got to Gary," one said.

I took the nearest exit and filled a gas can at a gas station near the Interstate. I went back and poured it into the van, then followed them back to the station and filled them up so we could continue on to Gary.

...

Financing remained the biggest issue. We had less fan support than we needed. Our attendance averaged about two hundred per game. Sometimes we looked up at the bleachers, and there were only maybe twenty-five to fifty people sitting in the stands. If we got three or four hundred, we'd be happy. I took the position that if I had one person in the audience, I had a guest. I had to put on the best show for that one guest. That philosophy gave me the courage to keep going.

I told the players to use their God-given gifts. They may not be able to dunk the ball like the men, but if they were good at ball handling, I wanted to see them dribble between their legs and pass behind their backs and run-and-gun up and down the floor.

"I don't want any hot-dogging," I said. "But if God gave you a gift, use whatever talent you have. We want

The Vision

to entertain people."

They did their jobs. Our games were so exciting. Both teams scored more than one hundred points in every one. From the tip of the ball, the players were gone. It was like a fireworks show every night. That's what audiences liked about them.

...

Our stand-by player joined us in Minnesota to replace the player with the broken ankle. As promised, her parents had driven her there from their home in Wisconsin. Since she was a back-up player, I made sure the coach put her in the game that night so her parents could watch her play. She played a great ball game. I think she scored in double figures with a lot of assists. Her parents beamed with pride. After the game, she hugged her parents, hopped in the van, and came with us.

...

After Minnesota we were out of money. We canceled our trip to Omaha. By the end of the tour we had lost around ten thousand dollars. I had bought gas and had to buy some food, but there were also little things I had never considered. I had told the players they didn't need any money. All they had to do was eat, sleep, ride, and play. But along the way they needed a little spending money for such items as soap, toothpaste, and make-up. Sometimes the girls and coaches would go out to the movies, and I paid for that, too. All in all, the tour cost more than I had figured on because of the lack of game profits.

I had used my brother's American Express card, and I couldn't pay him back.

He accepted that. "If you get it, pay me," he said. "If not, don't worry about it."

I wanted to quit the whole thing then. I was still sleeping on the floor in the basement at my sister's. I had no other place to stay and no job. Then, I thought, I'm going to get me a job. I found one at Kraft Tool in the 18th and Vine Streets Jazz District in Kansas City, Missouri. The owner's name was Ron Meyer. I'd been working at Kraft Tool about six weeks when Ron called me back to his office.

I thought what have I done wrong? I didn't realize that God was working through Ron to keep me going.

In spring 1993 the Kansas City *Star* published a write-up about the league I planned to start, but I gave it little thought. However, Ron had seen it and paid attention.

When I got to Ron's office, he said, "I want to encourage you."

"About what?" I asked.

"I read the article in the *Star*. I think it's a wonderful thing that you're trying to do. But if you're going to own a business, you have to give it 110 percent of your time."

I nodded.

"You're a good worker," he said. "You're the best worker I've got. But this is not going to work. I'm telling you as an owner: If you want to, go and give it everything you've got. If it doesn't work out, you can

The Vision

come back here. There'll be a job for you."

That gave me a boost.

After work that same evening my sister Linda Mae Bell told me I had a message. "A woman from *Women's Sports and Fitness Magazine* called."

"What'd she want?"

"They want to run an article about the league. She said to call whatever time you got in."

Somebody cared! Now, I was fired up and ready to go again. I decided to go forward even though I was in big debt with no major business support. I stayed at Kraft tool until the winter of 1993. One day I went into Ron's office. "I'm going to take you up on your offer," I said.

Brenda and I moved into our own apartment, and I started planning the 1993 season.

...

In March 1993 I looked at a map to choose cities for the franchises. I settled on the cities and where each team would play.

Team	**Venue**
Beatrice, Nebraska	Beatrice City Auditorium
Cedar Rapids, Iowa	Coe College
Kansas City, Kansas	Metropolitan Community College /Olathe Salvation Army
Kansas City, Missouri	Rockhurst College (now Rockhurst University)
Quincy, Illinois	City Auditorium
Tulsa, Oklahoma	High school gym

We assigned players from the tryouts in Milwaukee to some of the teams. I sent news releases and bought ads in newspapers in those cities asking for volunteer general managers, coaches, and more players. Mail came in like crazy. When I interviewed people I told them there'd be no money up front. They'd have to work on commission. But they'd be pioneers. Many of them wanted to be part of it.

I began by looking for a general manager and coaches for the Kansas City franchises. I heard from Connie Turnipseed. She had seen the ad and was interested in being part of the new league.

I had known Connie when I played football in Iowa. She had asked for my autograph after a game there. I signed one for her and one for her friend, and we all went out to dinner together. From there we became good friends. After that I moved to Wisconsin, and we lost contact until she saw the ad. I didn't realize who she was until she reminded me. Connie came aboard and ran the league operation. She also sold tickets at games and set up press conferences.

For the other franchises I got the best people for general managers. They ran operations the way I wanted them run. They set up the practice and game facilities. I got great coaches, too. One was Joe C. Meriweather, who coached the Missouri team. At 6-feet, 10-inches tall Joe had been a star center at Southern Illinois University. He played for the NBA between 1975 and 1985 with the Houston Rockets, Atlanta Hawks, New Orleans Jazz, New York Knicks, and Kansas City

Kings. He won the bronze medal as a member of the U.S. National Team in the 1974 FIBA World Championship. Jamie Collins, who also coached at Avila University in Kansas City, Missouri, coached the Kansas City, Kansas, team in 1993 and in 1994 joined Joe C. as the co-head coach of the Kansas City Mustangs.

I also met a couple named Debbie and Pee Wee Summers, who officiated women's basketball games for Kansas State University and the University of Missouri. I hired them to oversee all the WWBA officials, because they had connections with other officials throughout the Midwest. Debbie was a Godsend to me. She and her husband owned a State Farm Insurance agency in Kansas City, Kansas. Debbie became the league's vice president and, later, president. She also officiated some of the games with her husband. Pee Wee was the top supervisor over all the league officials. He set up the officials for all the WWBA games.

We held tryouts for players in each franchise area. Before tryouts in Kansas City, I did an interview with the Kansas City *Star*. "Women's basketball has really changed directions over the years," I told the reporter. "We feel at this point, with the following of the women's NCAA Final Four, the time is right to reintroduce America to professional women's basketball."

I explained my hope to give young women with basketball experience an opportunity to stay at home to continue to play, instead of having to go overseas. "We feel like we can field the very best Division I and

Division II players that the states have to offer," I continued in the interview. "We're talking about highly competitive and exciting basketball."

The article ran on Thursday, March 11, 1992. The publicity helped attract players for the tryouts held the next Saturday at Penn Valley Community College.

I always tried to get a high school or college player who the city could identify with. And all the players we got were glad to be playing ball. The teams had no mascots like college teams, but we did have five or six little girls between the ages of three and six who dressed up in costumes. The Mustangs, for example, had kids dressed up like cowgirls to keep families entertained.

Everyone who joined us was happy to be part of the league. They saw a new awareness and acceptance of the league. They could see that something was happening, and they wanted to be part of it.

...

I knew that once the league started, people would compare the men's game with the women's game. I was determined to put on a good show with play worthy of dedicated fans. But there were differences in men's and women's size and strength. Not many women grow to 6-feet, 6-inches. Not many can press three hundred pounds. Not many can dunk the ball. But basketball is basketball. I knew that women could play guns-a-blazin' as hard as men. And I knew we had a group of women who loved basketball and loved to compete.

Kansas City Mustangs Coach Joe C. Meriweather agreed with me. He had coached high school girls, as

The Vision

well as men. "The only difference I found is the girls can't dunk," Meriweather told *USA Today* at the end of the 1994 season. "Other than that, they can do anything the guys can do. What I find so exciting with the ladies is so much ball control. There's really nice finesse shooting. And (the game) is physical."

And the Game Goes On

Chapter 5
Full Court Press

In the season opener of the inaugural season of the WWBA on April 10, 1993, at Rockhurst College (now Rockhurst University) in Kansas City, Missouri, Maurtice Ivy #43 at wing for the Nebraska Xpress got in position to box out the defender. Her team's shooting guard hurled a trey. The shot missed, but Maurtice was right there for the offensive rebound. She scored and hustled to the opposite end of the floor ready to play defense.

Sweat dripped from her forehead, and her muscles burned from the intense effort of one of the closest games she had ever played. It was one of those games where a mistake could cost the game. Energy in the arena was high.

Under the Kansas City Mustangs' goal, forward Sarah Campbell #33 heard her point guard yell a play. Sarah waited on the block and took an inside pass, bounced the ball with a drop step toward the basket, and, anticipating a foul, went up strong to nail a bank shot. She drew the foul, and as the players from both teams lined up for her free-throw, they bent down, rested their hands on their knees, and gulped air, relishing even a few seconds of needed rest. Even though Sarah felt fatigue, the adrenaline pumping through her body helped her focus. She made the extra point.

If you watched the fans, you'd think they were watching a tennis match instead of a basketball game. The bucket-to-bucket showdown seemed like the Shootout at the OK Corral. It was a most exciting game, and it boded well for the new league.

Both teams had strong leaders, and Maurtice and Sarah wouldn't let either team give up. Both teams played with intensity that matched anything the men's NBA offered.

Maurtice had played college basketball for the University of Nebraska-Lincoln from 1984 to 1988. As a forward/guard swing player she had been a three-time, first-team All-Big Eight selection, averaging 19.2 points per game. She was the first female Husker to score more than 2,000 points. She also was the first Nebraska player to earn Big Eight Player of the Year honors, which she earned after the team won the 1988 conference tournament championship. Despite her 5-foot, 9-inch height, she was one of the best rebounders and shot blockers in the school's history. You'd think she was 6-feet, 9-inches tall. She blew me away.

Sarah, a 5-foot, 11-inch forward from the University of Missouri with a 64 percent field goal percentage,

The Vision

played on the 1985 USA Basketball William Jones Cup team and was a first-team All-America selection. This was the caliber of players we recruited for the WWBA.

The game was tied 89-89 at the end of regulation play and tied again 110-110 after the first two-minute overtime. The score was 119-119 after the second overtime. As the third overtime ticked to a close, the Kansas City Mustangs hit a jump shot to bring the score to 126-127. The Nebraska Xpress hit a trey as the clock ran out and won the game 126-130.

The women were exhausted, but they hadn't quit. They gave it all on the floor. Maurtice had 61 points for the game, and Sarah knocked in 54.

Fans jumped to their feet, and a roar of applause exploded. One of the fans told a reporter from the Kansas City *Star,* "I'm from Los Angeles, and I've seen the (NBA) Lakers play many games. Not one of them was as exciting as this one! If there's another game while I'm here, you can be assured you will find me there. I'll pay to see these girls anytime."

As fans applauded all over the arena, I got the greatest feeling. My chest felt like it was full of air. Something special was happening. And I knew the hand of God was involved.

...

The Nebraska Xpress and Kansas City Mustangs match-up was part of regular season play that started with six teams divided into two conferences. The American conference teams included the Nebraska Xpress in Beatrice, Nebraska; the Missouri Mustangs in

Kansas City, Missouri; and the Oklahoma Cougars in Tulsa, Oklahoma. The World Conference teams were the Kansas Crusaders in Kansas City, Kansas; the Iowa Unicorns in Cedar Rapids, Iowa; and Illinois Knights in Quincy, Illinois.

The teams each practiced twice a week and played a fifteen-game schedule on Saturday nights. The away teams left early in the morning on Saturday and rode in vans for as much as eight or nine hours to the games. They spent the night and returned home on Sunday, sometimes very late at night. After each game the managers called me, the other coaches, and the media to report scores and stats. Money from each game stayed with the teams.

...

Prior to home openers for other franchises, I held news conferences in those cities to introduce the teams and show off the logos designed by Jim Potter and the team T-shirts designed by Sid Messer.

At the Nebraska Xpress news conference, for example, Tiny Hovet, who served as the head coach, as well as the chief administrator of player personnel that year, joined me in Beatrice on the Wednesday before the Xpress's home opener on April 17, 1993. We had already talked with some city officials, and Mayor Dave Maurstad seemed optimistic about the league.

"(The local team) can only be a good situation for us," Mayor Maurstad told Bruce M. Viergutz of the Beatrice *Daily Sun*. "I hope the community and surrounding area will support the team."

The Vision

As it happened, along with serving as mayor, he also officiated high school and junior college basketball. He told us that high school girls' basketball enjoyed plenty of enthusiastic fans in the town. That boded well for our new league.

At the news conference, I told the reporters, "We've got very good support from Beatrice officials. We felt this would be a better location than Omaha or Lincoln, where there are lots of other things going on, and they might not accept or appreciate a franchise and league like this."

I again mentioned that the WWBA gave female players a chance to play in the United States instead of overseas after their college careers ended. "We know it's going to take time, but we're going to do what it takes to keep them in the USA."

Tiny Hovet chimed in about the quality of players fans would see. "We're very pleased with the overall play of the ladies," he told the Beatrice *Daily Sun*. "You'd be very surprised how skilled these players are in a one-on-one situation."

...

The Beatrice, Nebraska, home opener for the Nebraska Xpress was a rout for the Xpress over the Iowa Unicorns 151-111. As would be the case throughout the years of the league, fan support was remarkable. Attendance at the Beatrice City Auditorium was nearly 400. The game was so exciting that lots of fans bought $25 season tickets. Regular season single-game tickets were $5.

Three dedicated fans included Dorwin Ducket and Paul Redwine and his wife, all from Beatrice. Ducket told the Beatrice *Daily Sun,* "I've lived in California and Arizona. I've seen the Lakers, Clippers, and Suns play, but (this game) was as good of a show as the NBA could put on."

He also talked about his purchase of a season ticket. "(This) one game was worth the price of a season ticket," he told *Sun-Times* reporter Jane White. "I'm ready to go again. This is something our community needs to support. I'd like to see this get going."

Paul Redwine agreed. He told the Sun-Times, "This game was great entertainment. It's the best Saturday night I've had in a long time."

...

In Cedar Rapids, Iowa, Larry Fields, head coach of the Iowa Unicorns, and I held a news conference at the local YMCA. Larry was well-known in the area, due to his career there as a middle school basketball coach. At the conference, I promoted the upcoming Unicorns' home opener against the Oklahoma Cougars at LaSalle High School.

As we did in other cities, we tried to get players with ties to the community. In Cedar Rapids, we got 5-foot, 11-inch Robin Becker, a forward who had played high school basketball at Jefferson High School and college ball at St. Ambrose University in nearby Davenport, Iowa, where she was twice named an NAIA All-America player. She joined Angie Eichhorst, who had played at Marion High School, just a short drive down the road from Cedar Rapids. Angie was a standout at Indiana State University in Terre Haute, Indiana. While she played for the Unicorns, she also served as assistant basketball coach at St. Ambrose under head coach Robin Becker.

The entire team had not been named at the time of the news conference, but the Unicorns players also included three players from Mount Mercy University in Cedar Rapids: Robin Bragg, Joan Steffen, and Julie Ganahl. Robin earned Division II All-America honors. Point guard Joan Steffen set an NAIA assist record (328) and became the Midwest Classic Conference Player of the Year in 1991. Julie Ganahl was an assistant coach at Mount Mercy and an elementary schoolteacher in Cedar Rapids. They were joined by Steph Schueler and Katie Abrahamson, who played on our tour in the summer of 1992. Katie had been a star at Washington High School in Cedar Rapids.

An outstanding Iowa player from Drake University, Jan Jensen, who had been the NCAA Division I Player of the Year there in 1991, could not join the Unicorns full-time because of her duties as assistant coach at Drake. "I want to do everything I can to help establish an American women's professional basketball league," she told the Cedar Rapids *Gazette*, "but my job will always come first."

I was proud to announce so many players with ties to the community.

"All we ask is give these girls an opportunity," I told sportswriter Bob Hilton of the *Gazette*. "Don't judge them until you see them. We think when you see them, you won't be disappointed."

I explained how we decided on Cedar Rapids for our Iowa franchise. We at first wanted to play at the Drake University field house in Des Moines, Iowa. However, the cost would have been too high to keep admission prices affordable for low-income fans. We also looked at Kirkwood, Regis, and LaSalle before choosing Cedar Rapids. But, we assured the reporters, we were in Cedar Rapids to stay.

"You won't wake up one morning and find this franchise gone," I told the *Gazette*. "The game's going on, whether there are twenty people in the seats or two thousand. The people behind this league are people who are willing to stay with it. They don't expect it to happen overnight."

I also encouraged community participation, both as fans and local sponsors. "We want to see the fans more excited than we are," I said. "We want the community happy. We want the community involved."

...

Once the schedule started, I traveled to a different home site every week. One week I'd be in Kansas City, the next I'd be in Iowa. I made it a point to let people know that I was behind the league one hundred percent. I knew media would be at the games, and that some reporters might be negative. I wanted to assure them that the WWBA was no fly-by-night operation. It was for real.

At the games I observed the attendance and

watched the games. I went around talking to fans, asking how their family was being treated and what could be improved. I was always looking for ways to make things better the next time.

Once I completed the circuit, I called a coaches' meeting in a conference room at the Holiday Inn on the Country Club Plaza in Kansas City, Missouri. I was convinced we had to put the best product on the floor. When the coaches assembled, I told them, "I want you to let the women use their abilities. Let them play their game."

The coaches nodded.

"But no showboating," I said. "Make them do it professionally."

After that I started the circuit over again and went back to previous sites. My coaches' meeting paid off. The game really opened up. The players were like wild stallions going out of the gate. In one Kansas City Mustangs game, Lisa Braddy executed a behind the back pass to Robbie Garcia. Then Robbie shot a three-pointer. The crowd went nuts. That surprised me, but not Robbie. She was ready for it.

...

In another game in Beatrice, Nebraska, two of our players really shone. Maurtice Ivy was a 5-foot, 11-inch guard/forward swing player. She had played college ball at the University of Nebraska, and was one of the best rebounders and shot blockers. Lisa Long had played at the University of Iowa. They developed a bit of a rivalry on the tour. From the start of the Beatrice game, you'd think you had Michael Jordan and Magic Johnson in there. One player would make a move that looked like a lay-up, but she'd dish it to a team-mate. On the next possession the other would make a spin move and shoot. Maurtice faked a move to the goal, but pulled back and shot the ball.

When Lisa Long jumped she could put her hand up by the rim like a guy. She could dunk an Alley Oop like an NBA player. When she did that, I turned to Larry Fields and asked, "Is she human?"

This is the type of quality skills these women had.

...

As the season progressed, the Nebraska Xpress commanded the league. With four games left in regular season play, they topped all teams with a 9-2 win/loss record, followed by the Kansas Crusaders and Missouri Mustangs, both with 7-4 records. That didn't stop the Missouri Mustangs from coming to Beatrice, Nebraska, ready to win in their second match-up of the year. The Nebraska Xpress had only seven players available to play, with Karen Jennings and Diane Foli absent. That, plus the fact that Nebraska got off to a slow start may have contributed to the Missouri win 114-110.

"The shots just weren't going in early," Xpress Coach Janet Reiser told the Beatrice *Daily Sun*. "And Missouri was ready for us."

But the Xpress didn't go down without a fight. Maurtice Ivy led Nebraska with 34 points, followed by Renee Dozier with 26, Sandy Skradski with 20, and Melissa Sanford with 17.

The Vision

I was in Beatrice for the game, and I was so proud of the players. What impressed me most, though, was the fan support. The town was a great market for the Xpress. On a scale of one to ten for attendance, Beatrice would get a ten. And Miami, Oklahoma, home of the Oklahoma Cougars, would rate a nine.

...

We were blessed that we got media coverage that season. Publicity was important for the new league, and the Kansas City *Star* sports editor Dale Bye sent a young reporter named Terrance Harris to cover our games and players. At first he seemed a bit negative about what we were trying to accomplish. But at the end, thank God, we won him over.

"There definitely was some skepticism," Harris said years later.

Harris covered high school sports for the *Star* during the school year. He had nothing to cover in summer, so his editor assigned him to the WWBA.

"Lightning sold Bye on the league, and Bye made me cover it," Harris said. "It was part of my summer hustle. In today's world, with our ability to research people the way we can now, I don't know if we would have messed with Lightning. But I have to give him credit. He's a pretty bright guy. He had an idea and a vision, and he made it work."

Harris was impressed with the quality of WWBA play. "The basketball was really good," he said. "A lot of his players would have been playing for the WNBA if it had existed then."

I was pretty excited with the first interviews with the Kansas City *Star,* and sportscasters at Channels 4 and 5 in the same city. They gave us great publicity that spurred awareness of the league's existence. I knew we had great players. And Harris understood my vision to create a top-level professional league for women.

"Lightning created the road map for the WNBA," Harris said. "He showed what a women's professional basketball league could be if it had the resources to pull it off."

...

The Nebraska Xpress led by Maurtice Ivy posted the best overall record for the season at 15-2. The Oklahoma Cougars had the worst at 3-12. Evette Ott of the Kansas Crusaders was named Most Valuable Player for the season.

1993 WWBA Regular Season Results

American Conference:

Team	Win/Loss Record
Nebraska Xpress	13-2
Missouri Mustangs	10-5
Oklahoma Cougars	3-12

World Conference:

Team	Win/Loss Record
Illinois Knights	10-5
Kansas Crusaders	5-10
Iowa Unicorns	4-11

At the end of the season, the team with the best record in each conference got a bye in the first round of the playoffs. The other two teams in each conference played each other in a "best two out of three" round. Of these four teams, the two with the best records played the first playoff games at home. Then play continued at the other teams' venues. If a third game was needed, the teams returned to the first city. Winners of that round played the top teams in the best three out of five games to advance to the championship best-of-five series.

...

In the first game of the playoffs, the Iowa Unicorns beat the Missouri Mustangs 118-103 at Rockhurst College. Reported attendance was 150. Missouri dominated the first half with a 13-0 run in the second quarter and team-highs of 19 points by forward Sarah Campbell and 18 points by forward Danielle Shareef. The Mustangs led 65-54 at the half.

But Iowa started the third quarter with its own 13-0 run and tied the game at 67 before Missouri regained the lead. Still, Iowa outscored Missouri 32-18 and held their opponents to 6 of 22 field goals. In contrast, Iowa was 10 of 21 from the field and pulled ahead with three consecutive treys. With time running out in the third period, forward Robin Becker of the Unicorns scored the last 6 points to lead 86-83.

In the fourth quarter Iowa power forward Lisa Long's strong inside moves added 17 points toward her game high total of 42.

"Once Lisa gets in that groove, she's pretty tough to stop," Iowa Coach Larry Fields told the Kansas City *Star*. "I think she intimidated the Missouri team some."

Along with Lisa Long, leading scorers for Iowa included Diana Vines with 27 points and Robin Becker with 25 points.

The Missouri Mustangs won the next two games over the Iowa Unicorns (98-93 and 117-112 OT). Missouri's Sarah Campbell scored an incredible WWBA single-game record 62 points, and Iowa's Lisa Long led her team with 37.

...

In the first round of the other playoff series, the Kansas Crusaders beat the Oklahoma Cougars 92-77. The two teams were tied at 18 at the end of the first period. In the second, however, the Crusaders outscored the Cougars 22-13. Kansas led 40-31 at the half.

Oklahoma brought the score within 6 in the third quarter, 65-59. But the fourth quarter went to the Crusaders, who hit 27 points to Oklahoma's 18 to bring the final score to 92-77. The game high scorer was Stacy Truitt, forward for Kansas, who scored 28 points. Carla Hough led the Cougars with 17.

...

The remaining playoff in the first round pitted the Kansas Crusaders against the Oklahoma Cougars. The teams were tied at 20 points each at the end of the first quarter. That's when Crusaders' Coach Jamie Collins started yelling.

"I couldn't believe we were tied after one quarter," the coach told the Kansas City *Kansan*. "I yelled at them for their play on defense. If they didn't play defense, they had to sit down."

The next quarter saw the Kansas team light up. They outscored their opponents 32-16 for a 52-36 half-time lead. By the fourth quarter, the Oklahoma players' legs were gone, and they were emotionally out of the game. They scored only 6 points to Kansas's 33 for a final score of 114-64.

As the Crusaders headed for the second round of the playoffs against the Missouri Mustangs, Coach Jamie Collins had some words for her players.

"We're just going to go out and kick butt," she told the Kansas City *Kansan*. "We will play good defense and dig down deep emotionally. And anybody who doesn't play defense can sit here beside me on the bench."

...

In the second round the Nebraska Xpress beat the Illinois Knights 166-129, setting a WWBA scoring record. The Xpress also won the second game 127-115. The Kansas Crusaders beat the Missouri Mustangs in two (121-97 and 109-99).

...

The best-of-five championship series pitted the Kansas Crusaders against the Nebraska Xpress in Beatrice, Nebraska. The Xpress was playing without one of their best players. Karen Jennings left the team earlier in the week to join a professional women's league in France.

"I guess maybe I'm being a bit optimistic, but I really think that we can still pull it out without Karen," Xpress Coach Janet Ereiser told the Kansas City *Star*. "She will definitely be missed, but I still believe that the caliber of players we still have is very high."

Still, Kansas was considered the underdog in the match-up. Nebraska had won all three regular season games against them.

"This is a whole new season as far as I'm concerned," Evette Ott told the *Star* before the first

The Vision

game. "I think that we have really come together as a team during the playoffs, which makes us a much different and better team."

In the first game the Kansas Crusaders beat the Nebraska Xpress 125-119. Nebraska was up by 13 at the end of the first quarter 32-25. By half-time, though Kansas led 59-53. In the second half the Crusaders relied on defense and rebounding to win. Leading scorers for Kansas included Stacy Truitt with 29 points and Evette Ott with 25. Yvette Tunley scored 13, and Alesia Prince, Kay Kay Hart, and Terrilyn Johnson each made 10.

Sandy Skradski of Nebraska had a game-high 36 points, and Renee Dozier had 31. Also in double figures for the Xpress were Melissa Stanford with 23 and Maurtice Ivy with 15. The win was the first for a visiting team on the Xpress's home court.

...

The Xpress bounced back in the second game in Beatrice 118-100. The Crusaders came back to Kansas City for the third game held at Penn Valley Community College in Kansas City, Missouri. The Crusaders won the third game 111-96, behind five players who each scored in double figures. Evette Ott led them with a game-high 24.

Defense might have been the key. It was the first time the Xpress scored fewer than 100 points all season. The league leading team in scoring averaged 130 points per game during the regular season.

"It was a combination of great second half defense

and poor shooting by Nebraska," Coach Jamie Collins told the Kansas City *Kansan*. "We just cranked it up on defense. They weren't hitting their shots, and I credit that to our defense.

Unfortunately, during the game leading scorer Evette Ott sprained her right ankle coming down on someone's foot after pulling in a rebound. She was walking on it, but her coach knew it would be day-to-day to see if she could play the next game five days later.

"It will take horses to keep her back," Coach Collins told the *Kansan*. "She's too much of a competitor."

The Crusaders win forced the Xpress to a must-win fourth game.

"Our victory took a lot of the pressure off of us," Coach Collins told the *Kansan*. "Now the pressure is on Nebraska. They have to win or the series is over. It would be really sweet to finish it out at home in front of our fans, who have followed us since April."

In the fourth game, also played at Penn Valley Community College in Kansas City, Missouri, the Crusaders played without Evette Ott. The ankle just wouldn't hold. So Coach Collins started reserve forward Robbie Garcia in Evette's place.

"I was nervous about not having Evette," Coach Collins told the *Kansan*. "But I knew Robbie could score. I had super confidence in Robbie."

Robbie delivered with a game high 26. She wasn't the only Kansas scorer in double digits. Stacy Truitt had 22, Maryann Mitts had 15, Yvette Tunley had 13,

The Vision

and Alesia Prince had 10. Other Kansas players included Lisa Braddy, Joy Champ, Kay Kay Hart, Terrilyn Johnson, Erica Miller, and Maryann Mitts.

"We all knew we had to score more without Evette," Robbie Garcia told the *Kansan*. "Everybody stepped up and played harder."

And, as they had all season, they played as a team. "Robbie had fire in her eyes," teammate Stacy Truitt told the *Kansan*. "She came out and had the hot hand. I don't mind giving up points and setting picks for somebody shooting better than I am."

Both teams fought to the wire. The third quarter was key to the win. The Crusaders outscored the Xpress 33-23 (including 11 points by Robbie Garcia) to lead 77-67 at the end of the period. But, as they say, the Fat Lady hadn't yet sung.

In the last quarter, the Xpress came roaring back. With 42 seconds left in the game, Nebraska's Maurtice Ivy hit a three-pointer, and Sandy Skradski finished a three-point play to bring the Xpress within two 98-96.

As seconds ticked off the clock, the Crusaders' Robbie Garcia got the ball and pulled up for a three-point jumper that missed. Nebraska rebounded. But Robbie was so mad at herself, she stole the ball back. She drove to the bucket and hit a lay-up to bring the score to 100-96 with 10 seconds left. Nebraska's Renee Dozier hit a layup at the other end, but time ran out. The Crusaders took the crown 100-98.

"I thought I was going to have a heart attack at the end," Crusaders' Coach Collins told the *Kansan*. We wanted a high percentage shot, not a three-point shot. That's how coaches end up retiring."

Leading scorers for Nebraska included Renee Dozier with 24, Maurtice Ivy and Sandy Skradski with 20 each, and Lisa Kenkel with 15. Their teammates included Brook Benson, Diane Foli, and Trudi Veerhusen.

Evette Ott of Kansas won the WWBA Most Valuable Player award, even though she didn't play in the championship game. Maurtice Ivy of Nebraska was MVP runner-up. The WWBA also honored Nebraska's Melissa Sanford as Showtime Player and Missouri's Sarah Campbell as WWBA Scoring Champion. Kansas Crusaders' Coach Jamie Collins was named WWBA Coach of the Year.

Every game in the playoff rounds and championship series was fast and furious. All the coaches reported that fans gave standing ovations. As fans left the arenas, they congratulated players on the great games. Words can't describe what was going on. You needed to be there to see it. These girls played so hard, you'd think they were being paid millions of dollars. They weren't. In fact, sometimes they weren't paid at all. But the fans seemed to enjoy the game to the point where they thought they got something for their money.

As the season ended, joy filled my heart, because the fans were accepting the league.

Chapter 6
Benched

Heading into the 1994 season, lack of money again posed a major obstacle. The league lost another $100,000 during the 1993 season. I wanted to keep the league going, but how? I was beginning to think I couldn't do it any more. I prayed, "Lord, if I don't get some help here, I can't go on. I need to find support or something major."

God answered with the idea of looking for sponsors for the league. I decided to try to reach Michael Jordan and Magic Johnson through their foundations, but I couldn't get to them. I did talk to a couple of their agents, who told me that neither Michael nor Magic would be interested. Not to be discouraged, I called the NBA and asked for Commissioner David Stern. His secretary advised me to talk to Val Ackerman, director of business affairs.

Val had been one of the first female athletes to get an athletic scholarship from the University of Virginia. She started all four years on the women's basketball team, serving three years as team captain. She was the first Virginia basketball player to score 1,000 points. After college, she played one season of professional basketball in France.

I thought she'd be open to a women's professional league that let Americans play in their home country.

I called her and told her the main points of our philosophy. I told her we let the players play their own game. I told her we played in summer, unlike previous women's leagues, so our only professional competition for sports fans was baseball. I told her we used man-to-man defense and a 24-second shot clock to keep the game moving.

I showed her our uniforms with long shorts instead of sexier short shorts, because we wanted the audience to watch the game, not ogle the players. I showed her our logos and explained how we planned to get the citizens of each franchise city to get behind their teams. I told her everything.

She seemed interested in the WBA, and I think she was really trying to help us at that point. But she said the NBA could be interested in sponsoring us only as a third or fourth party. She asked me to keep her informed. Sometime in the fall of 1993, I sent her some WBA hats and T-shirts. In a letter on NBA stationery dated December 2, 1993, she thanked me.

The Vision

OFFICE OF THE COMMISSIONER

December 2, 1993

Lightning Mitchell
Women's Basketball Association
4011 N. Bennington, #101
Kansas City, MO 64117

Dear Lightning:

    Just a note to say thanks for sending the hats and T-shirts and for providing us with an update on the WBA.

    Please keep us posted on the League's progress, and best of luck with the upcoming season.

Sincerely,

Valerie B. Ackerman
Director of Business Affairs

VBA:jf

I called Val three or four more times to update her on the progress of the league, as she had requested. I always came away from talking with her with hope that any day the NBA could come in and put in some big money. But I needed money right away. So then I got the idea to sell franchises to get funds for the 1994 season.

I put articles in the Kansas City *Star*, as well as newspapers in the cities the other WBA teams played in. In Kansas City, a man named Ron Lickteig called. He was district manager of Anacomp, a computer services and document management corporation. A league representative had tried to sell him on the idea of sponsoring the WBA. He and his wife Kimberly, who lived in Raytown, Missouri, attended a few games and saw the possibilities.

"My wife and I are interested in buying the Mustangs," he said. "The league will be good for everybody if it takes off."

We met, and I could do nothing but love both Ron and Kim. They had the same burning desire that I had to make the league a success. They bought the Kansas City franchise for $28,000 dollars.

"I look at this as an opportunity for girls to have dreams," Kim Lickteig told the Kansas City *Star Magazine* in March 1994. "As with anything that women have achieved, there were pioneers. In basketball, that's going to be us."

Later that summer her husband Ron Lickteig told *USA today*, "(The Kansas City Mustangs) are playing for

The Vision

future players. Probably the girls in junior high school now will be able to realize a full-time career in basketball."

The Missouri Mustangs became the Kansas City Mustangs. They moved their home games from Rockhurst College to Penn Valley Community College

Several players from the 1993 WBA champion Kansas Marauders moved to the Kansas City Mustangs that year. Evette Ott, Joy Champ, and Stacy Truitt had played competitive basketball for several years on the Kansas City Keys, an Amateur Athletic Union team. With the move to the Mustangs, the players rejoined other members of the Keys. Danielle Shareef, Stephanie Worthy, CeCi Harris, and Sarah Campbell of the Missouri WBA team had also played on the Keys.

"Everybody is just very excited, because this is how we thought it was going to be from the beginning," Danielle Shareef told the Kansas City *Star*. "We had played together for so long, and that's really how we wanted it to continue."

We knew the women had played together, but in 1993 we wanted to divide them up to create parity in the league. As we were reorganizing for the 1994 season, we had planned to move the Kansas Crusaders to Wichita, so we combined the players to what we thought would be the only team in the Kansas City area. Instead the Kansas team played as the Marauders that year and moved to Louisville, Kentucky, for the 1995 season.

Joe C. Meriweather came on as the head coach,

replacing Monica Jacobs, who had coached the Missouri Mustangs for the inaugural season. Team members looked forward to playing for him.

"We have a real strong team concept, and that's because that's what Joe C. stresses through his words and actions," Mustangs' forward Stephanie Worthy told the Kansas City *Star*. "You know with him you're going to get a fair shake, and I like that. If you bust your tail, he's going to recognize that."

...

I sold another franchise called the St. Louis RiverQueens. A woman named Margo Garvin called about that team. She was reluctant at first, but Ron Lickteig encouraged her. He did a lot to persuade her. She bought the St. Louis franchise for the same price Ron paid for Kansas City. The franchise sales gave me $56,000 for operating expenses for the 1994 season.

After tryouts held at Webster University in Webster Groves, Missouri, her team was loaded with high-quality players. Petra "Pistol Pete" Jackson had led the Salukis at Southern Illinois University-Carbondale to four twenty-win seasons between 1982 and 1986. She got the nickname because she reminded fans of NBA star "Pistol Pete" Maravich, who made a name for himself at Louisiana State University before going pro.

In Petra's college career the 5-foot, 8-inch guard scored 1,475 points, 641 rebounds, 268 assists, and 189 steals. In her senior year she earned a first-team All-Missouri Valley Conference selection and won the Paul Roberson Award from SIU. She twice earned All-

The Vision

Gateway Collegiate Athletic Conference honors.

According to Lorraine Kee in the St. Louis *Post-Dispatch* in Missouri, Jackson was considered the "finest clutch player ever at Southern Illinois University." In 1991 she was inducted into the university's Hall of Fame.

Petra regretted having passed up a chance to play professional basketball in The Netherlands – a regret she still harbored in 2016. So, when she learned there was a new women's professional team in St. Louis, she was ready to play.

"There was no hesitation about trying out," she said. "I was happy that those who didn't get a chance to see me play (in college) could see me now. And, I could continue being a role model for our young athletes. I was all for it, even if it mean little or no pay. I was 'game.'"

When she got to the tryouts, she recognized most of the other candidates. She either knew them or had played against them at some point in her career. "I didn't view any of them as rivals," she said. "Now we were coming all together to play as one. Plus, I'm a gamer, and when I lace up my war boots, it's on and I'm ready for battle."

Petra refused whatever payment there was for playing. She wanted to remain an amateur player. And she wanted to leave her mark.

"At this time, all the young people who would soon become stars had not yet overshadowed me. So (the WBA) was still giving me a little room to leave my mark on St. Louis and not be forgotten no matter how old I got."

Petra's teammates included Chris Aldridge, who was a first-team All-Gateway Conference selection from Eastern Illinois University. Karen Hermann had been a Kodak All-America selection at Washington University in St. Louis. Teresa Jackson previously played at the University of Nevada-Las Vegas. She had been the 1993 Big West Player of the Year. Lisa Sandbothe, who had played at the University of Missouri was a second-team All-Big Eight Conference honoree.

Other players for the RiverQueens included Rene Bishop from Southwest Missouri State University, Toynetta Clemons from Webster University, Niele Ivey from Notre Dame, Kristin Folkl from Stanford, Kim Rohlfing from Drake University, Charmin Smith from Stanford, Susan Wellman from Illinois State University, and Angie Lewis and Chris Shelton, who had both played at St. Louis University.

Head coach Bill Hanks was a teacher who coached high school freshman and sophomore boys' teams. His assistant coaches were Bob Weise and Randy Kriewall. Andrea Coffman's father Dale Coffman served as the team's general manager.

...

Throughout the league, the players were still happy to be playing ball. Robbie Garcia, who played for the Kansas Crusaders in 1993 and moved to the Kansas City Mustangs in 1994, always considered herself a trailblazer for a new generation of female athletes. She told the Kansas City *Star Magazine*, "I just love to play basketball. I hope the league can become like those overseas, where they fill up stadiums to see women's basketball. The important thing is to build a foundation, to get on our feet and grow. If we do that, we'll make a lasting imprint on basketball."

Although they had all played for free in 1993, in 1994 I wanted them to get paid. We wanted to pay each player $1,200 for fifteen games. Even with that, they couldn't quit their day jobs. On the Kansas City Mustangs, for example, Evette Ott was a sales representative for Cellular One. Stephanie Worthy was a teacher at Northeast Middle School. Lisa Braddy, who had 1,000-plus career points at the University of Kansas, as well as setting a Big Eight conference record of 686 assists, was an investigator for CRB credit service. And Joy Champ was a sales team leader at the AT&T Telemarketing Center.

Stacy Truitt and Robbie Garcia had additional pursuits. Stacy, who played women's basketball for three years as a Kansas Jayhawk, was finishing her education at the University of Kansas. Robbie Garcia was completing a long-distance doctorate in biomechanics and nutrition from Lasalle University in Mandeville, Louisiana, along with leading basketball clinics in Olathe, Kansas, and working at the Tomahawk Sports Dome in Shawnee, Kansas.

Players on other teams did the same kinds of things. On the RiverQueens, for example, Chris Aldridge drove a truck for United Parcel Service (UPS). Petra Jackson worked as a claims representative for Kemper Insurance. Teresa Jackson was a stay-at-home mother of a new baby. She had a two-and-one-half hour one-way commute to practices and games. Except for Toinetta Clemons, who was finishing her college days at Webster University, the rest of the squad, including Susan Wellman, Kim Rohlfing, Mary Helen Walker, and Andrea Coffman worked as basketball coaches at high schools in the St. Louis area.

With all their other obligations, they all wanted to play. "We were ballers and wanted to play," Petra Jackson said. "That's all that mattered to us."

Evette Ott of the Kansas City Mustangs echoed Petra's opinion. "Basketball is my outlet," she told the Kansas City *Star Magazine*. "I love it. I'm consumed by it."

Chapter 7
Motion

We hoped to improve attendance by trying three new markets for the 1994 season. The WBA added two expansion teams. One was the Memphis Blues. We moved the Illinois Knights from Quincy, Illinois, to St. Louis, Missouri, and they became the RiverQueens. We also added a team in Gary, Indiana, which became the Indiana Stars. They played in the Genesis Center.

Along with other fine players, the Memphis Blues signed two standouts Carolyn Blair, who played at Shelby State/Knoxville College, and Priscilla Sweeney, who played at Kansas State University.

The Indiana Stars picked up Terrilyn Johnson, who had played for the WBA's Kansas Crusaders, and Diana Vines, an outstanding player from DePaul University. Another somewhat local girl Becky Inman-Han had played high school basketball at Chesterton High School in Chesterton, Indiana, just four exits east of Gary on Interstate 94. She played college ball at William Penn University in Oskaloosa, Iowa.

Joining them were Sharon Carr from Loyola University, Jennifer Jones from Kansas State University, Nora McDonnagh from the University of Mississippi, Cassandra Pack from the University of Detroit, Lana Taylor from the University of Texas, and Sue Welenc, also from DePaul University.

The Oklahoma team that had played in Miami, Oklahoma, moved to Tulsa, Oklahoma, and changed their name from the Cougars to the Flames. The Iowa Unicorns changed their name to the Iowa Twisters. Only the Nebraska Xpress stayed the same.

For the 1994 season we changed the names of the conferences to the American and National conferences. At this time, we dropped the word *World* from the league name. I thought the Women's Basketball Association (WBA) sounded stronger. With all the changes, we ordered new team logos with a more professional look.

I announced all these changes and displayed the new team logos at a news conference at the Adam's Mark Hotel in Kansas City, Missouri, to kick off the new season.

"This is not to say that we weren't pleased with our first season in any way," I told the reporters. "We just felt that we needed to make some changes to give a more professional image to the WBA."

Ron Lickteig was at the news conference. He told the Kansas City *Star*, "I'm excited about being part of the WBA. I look forward to being involved in women's basketball."

The Vision

WBA Franchise Logos

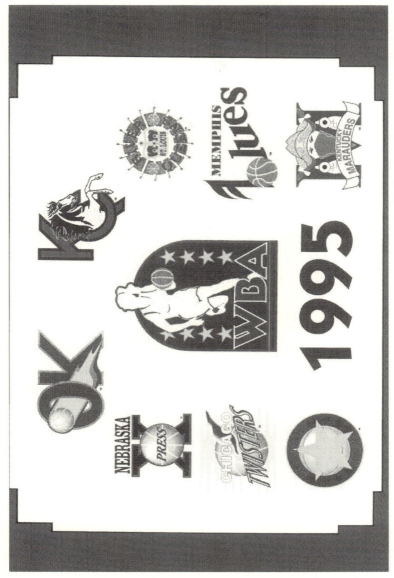

New, professional logos were designed for the WBA's 1994 and 1995 seasons.

...

The Iowa Twisters 1994 season home opener against the Kansas Marauders held at the Teikyo Marycrest Activities Center continued the exciting play we'd seen during the previous season. The lead changed hands several times during the game. But the play for both teams was a bit sloppy. Iowa started the game making eight of their first eleven shots. But for the entire game, Twisters' shooting hit just 37 of 102 field goal tries. Kansas made only 37 of 99.

"This is the first game, and we need to work on some things," Twisters' Coach Larry Fields told the Kansas City *Star*. "It might have been some opening night jitters."

Iowa's Lisa Long started the game with three quick buckets. Her team led 7-2. But the Twisters could never manage more than a six-point lead throughout the game. Iowa led 23-21 at the end of the first quarter and 47-45 at the half. Iowa again led at the end of the third quarter 78-75. But it was the last two minutes of the game that told the tale. Kansas's Jean Bacon scored 8 points in the final 12 minutes. Her teammate Denise Ballenger also made 8 points in the quarter.

As the clock ran down, the Twisters' Robin Becker was fouled three times and hit all six shots to give Iowa the lead 104-98 with 1:30 left. The Marauders Lori Hogan made a two-point shot. Then Kansas's Denise Ballenger took over. She hit a trey with 47 seconds left in the game. The Twisters fouled her three times during the time left, and she made five of six from the line to win the game for Kansas 110-106.

The Vision

"Our pressure defense broke down a little bit, and we got helter-skelter at the end," Twisters Coach Larry Fields told the *Quad-City Times.* "We should have held the ball and looked for a better shot."

Lisa Long, Robin Becker, Angie Eichorst, and Keesha Brooks led the Twisters with strong offense. Lisa Long had 29 points, along with a double-double of 26 rebounds. Robin Becker also scored a double-double with 24 points and 12 boards. Angie Eichorst contributed 25, despite making only 5 of 16 three-point tries, and Keesha Brooks hit 21. Notably, the Twisters' Ann Walker added excitement for the spirited crowd with 10 steals. Other Twisters players included Christa Arnold, Melinda Hippen, Jodi Sterling, and Ann Walker.

The Kansas Marauders had six players in double digits, with Dawn Stephens leading the way with 23 points and Annette Cole hitting her own double-double, adding 20 points and grabbing 14 rebounds. Also on the floor for the Marauders were Jean Bacon, Arneetrice Cobb, Kamiel Fisher, Lori Hogan, Gina Johnson, Rose McFarlan, Angie Oberbeck, Kim Steelandt, and Noel Wyatt.

The Kansas coach was pleased with the win. "This is our first look at anybody in the league," Coach Colleen Edwards told the *Quad-City Times.* "The girls did an outstanding job. Determination – that's what it was. They wanted to win."

...

Once the season got underway, a difficulty arose with the Memphis Blues. Once, the manaager suddenly changed the facility where the team was supposed to play. He told me they wanted too much money, but I knew that wasn't the problem.

"I'll come down there and look into it," I told him.

"I can handle it," he said. "I hate for you to drive so far for such a small problem."

He relayed other things to me, and I became very uncomfortable with him and his decisions. Some of his players called me, too. They said they had concerns with him, too. The guy kept complaining that there wasn't enough money and wanted me to send some more.

I went to one of the games unannounced, and the place was full of fans. So, why did he keep needing money? Something wasn't right. I let the manager go that night. The captain oversaw the team until I put the next manager in position a couple of days later. After that, the team had no further issues.

...

Play proceeded with an exciting season of basketball. All the games had high scores, with most games seeing 200 points or more being scored. In the first eight weeks, several players were recognized as Players of the Week. These included:

Week 1: Lynn Page, Oklahoma Flames, 31 pts
Week 2: Lisa Long, Iowa Twisters, 40 pts
Week 3: Sarah Campbell, Kansas City Mustangs, 37 pts
Week 4: Maurtice Ivy, Nebraska Xpress, 43 pts
Week 5: Diana Vines, Indiana Stars, 38 pts
Week 6: Helen Garrett, Oklahoma Flames, 40 pts

Week 7: Sarah Campbell, Kansas City Mustangs, 37 pts
Week 8: Chris Aldridge, St Louis RiverQueens, 27 pts

At the end of the season, the Kansas City Mustangs were undefeated (15-0), the only undefeated team in the league. The Nebraska Xpress and Memphis Blues both had the same record (10-5). But the Iowa Twisters (1-14) and Kansas Marauders (4-11) had struggled.

At the end of regular season play, the top three teams in each conference advanced to the playoffs. The two top teams in each conference (the Nebraska Xpress and the Kansas City Mustangs) each got a bye. Then the two second and third place teams played for the right to face the top teams in the championship series.

The Kansas City Mustangs looked like strong contenders for the title. "We have eleven girls who can play ball," Coach Joe C. Meriweather told *USA Today* before the second round of the playoffs. "When I bring girls in off the bench, we don't lose anything."

Franchise owner Ron Lickteig in the same article said, "In the second half, we outrun them. We just start blowing everybody out."

The Kansas City team got a bye in the first round of the playoffs.

So did the Nebraska Xpress, who had gone 10-5 in the regular season and won the American Conference. They were set to play two games in the second round with the Indiana Stars at Omaha Benson High School in Omaha, Nebraska. As we always tried to do, the Xpress had three players with ties to the Omaha area. Shannon

Struby had played at Millard South High School and Creighton University both in Omaha. Maurtice Ivy was a star at Omaha Central High School and the University of Nebraska. And Kelly Luenenborg had also played at Millard South and spent her college career at the University of Nebraska at Kearney.

1994 WBA Regular Season Results

American Conference:

Team	Win/Loss Record
Nebraska Xpress	10-5
Indiana Stars	8-7
Oklahoma Flames	3-6
Iowa Twisters	1-14

National Conference:

Team	Win/Loss Record
Kansas City Mustangs	15-0
Memphis Blues	10-5
St. Louis RiverQueens	9-6
Kansas Marauders	4-11

The players still weren't getting paid – at least not very often.

"Since we don't get a lot of fan support, it's difficult for them to pay us to play," forward Renee Dozier told the Omaha *World-Herald* before the playoffs. "Hopefully

The Vision

in the future that's something that will happen."

...

The Memphis Blues and Nebraska Xpress advanced to the best-of-five 1994 WBA Championship series. Memphis won the first game by a point 102-101. It's tough to lose by just one point, but that's all it takes. In the second game, Nebraska took Memphis 123-108. It looked like we were headed for an exciting conclusion to the season. And we were.

In the third game, played in the White Station High School gym in Memphis, the Blues won 138-128, playing themselves to a fourth – and possibly final – game of the series. The Blues dominated the game, expanding their lead to more than 20 points in the fourth quarter, never letting the Xpress come closer than 10 points during the final period.

Eight Memphis players shot in double figures with Terri Donald leading her team with 22 points and Carolyn Blair contributing 16. Both players had double-doubles with center Terri Donald grabbing 12 rebounds and Carolyn Blair bringing down 10.

Nebraska was handicapped by the fact that only seven players could make it to the game because of job conflicts. The ones who made it to the gym had traveled more than ten hours from Omaha the day of the game, and that trip probably took its toll, too.

"Without that extra assistance on the bench, it was hard for me to match up with some of the rotations," Xpress Coach Patrick Holston told Memphis's *The Commercial Appeal*.

The shallow bench put pressure on the Xpress's Maurtice Ivy. She rose to the occasion and scored 48 points and 17 rebounds during the game. But it wasn't enough, especially because of the Blues's center Terri Donald. She had her way in the paint, with shifts and twists and rebounding and passing. She struggled only with free throws, hitting only 8 of 15 shots.

The only relief for the Xpress came when Terri Donald was called for her fourth foul during the third quarter. Despite the Xpress's rally while she sat on the bench, she returned to the game and sealed Nebraska's fate.

"If we get the ball inside, I don't think (the Xpress) can stop any of our post players," she told *The Commercial Appeal*. "We were playing together, and I think that wore them down."

The Blues Assistant Coach Wanda Jones told *The Commercial Appeal*, "The game was not easy because they had pretty good players. We're going to keep the same game plan next time."

But, the Nebraska Xpress won the next two games 111-101 and 103-101 to take the championship. Maurtice Ivy of the Xpress was named Most Valuable Player.

At the end of the 1994 season, the WBA held an All-Star Game between the two conferences. It was a close, high-scoring game. The American Conference beat the National Conference 168-167.

1994 Playoff Results

WBA 1st Round Playoffs
Memphis 126, St. Louis 111
Memphis 122, St. Louis 110
Indiana 107, Oklahoma 91
Indiana 103, Oklahoma 91

WBA 2nd Round Playoffs
Kansas City 98, Memphis 94
Memphis 101, Kansas City 87
(winner determined by total points: Memphis 195, Kansas City 185)
Nebraska 99, Indiana 89
Nebraska 91, Indiana 87

1994 American Conference All-Stars

Head Coach: Larry Fields
Assistant Coaches: Carla Dudley and Mark McKinzie

Denise Ballenger	Iowa Twisters
Robin Becker	Iowa Twisters
Renee Dozier	Nebraska Xpress
Helen Garrett	Oklahoma Flames
Dixie Horn	Oklahoma Flames
Maurtice Ivy	Nebraska Xpress
Terrilyn Johnson	Indiana Stars
Lisa Long	Iowa Twisters
Lynn Page	Oklahoma Flames
Sandy Skradski	Nebraska Xpress
Nicole Tunsil	Iowa Twisters
Diana Vines	Indiana Stars

1994 National Conference All-Stars

Head Coach: Joe C. Merriweather
Assistant Coaches: Bill Hanks and Colleen Edwards

Chris Aldridge	St. Louis RiverQueens
Carolyn Blair	Memphis Blues
Arneetrice Cobb	Kansas Marauders
Sarah Campbell	Kansas City Mustangs
Robelyn Garcia	Kansas City Mustangs
Ceci Harris	Kansas City Mustangs
Petra Jackson	St. Louis RiverQueens
Evette Ott	Kansas City Mustangs
Danielle Shareef	Kansas City Mustangs
Priscilla Sweeney	Memphis Blues
Annie Taplin	Kansas Marauders
Stacey Truitt	Kansas City Mustangs
Susan Wellman	St. Louis RiverQueens
Stephanie Worthy	Kansas City Mustangs

Leading Scorers 1994 All-Star Game

American Conference

Player	Points
Maurtice Ivy	40
Diana Vines	30
Lisa Long	27
Terrilyn Johnson	24
Robin Becker	20
Renee Dozier	17
Sandy Skradski	10

National Conference

Player	Points
Petra Jackson	41
Sarah Campbell	45
Evette Ott	24
Chris Aldridge	22
Stacey Truitt	20
Stephanie Worthy	15

Chapter 8
Fast Break

At the end of the 1994 season, the league had lost even more money. About another $100,000. By then I had made up my mind that if something big didn't happen before we opened in 1995, I was going to shut down the league.

But first the idea came to me to reorganize the league and move a couple of teams to bigger markets. The WBA still consisted of eight teams, but two were in cities different from those in 1994. The Nebraska Xpress moved to Omaha. The Kansas Marauders became the Kentucky Marauders in Louisville.

Both the Indiana Stars and the Iowa Twisters were struggling. I was surprised about Iowa, since it was such a good atmosphere for women's college basketball at the time. But it was a hard market – a lot harder than I had thought. The first two years of the league, the fan support just wasn't there. We dropped the Iowa Twisters and moved the Indiana Stars to Chicago, who played at DePaul University. Chicago took on the name the Twisters. I also started a new team who played at the University of Minnesota in Minneapolis. We took the name from the defunct Indiana team and named them the Minnesota Stars.

In Chicago, Kandi Conda paid a $10,000 franchise deposit toward the $28,000 purchase price for the Twisters. Kandi also became the director of operations and general manager. That meant she was responsible for payment of players, administration, and staff, as well as advertising, marketing, sales, the venue, finances, programs, and all the rest of the day-to-day activities of the team.

She was a good supporter of the league and meant well in everything she did. She did everything she could to promote the team and did a great job with it. She was good people. If I could have had three or four more managers like her, I would have done it.

"I came on board to purchase the Chicago Twisters and give the players more stability," Kandi said.

She did a great job promoting her Chicago Twisters during the 1995 season. She got good media coverage, and local celebrities, community leaders, radio personalities, and professional football and basketball players attended their home games. She participated in such events as the Women's Black Expo in Chicago and took along several players to the booth to promote the team.

To announce her purchase of the team, she held a press conference at Michael Jordan's Restaurant, a multi-level sports bar on LaSalle Street in Chicago,

The Vision

Illinois. She was accompanied by former Milwaukee Bucks player Harvey Catchings, Olympian Willye White, Jim Rose of Channel 7 in Chicago, and team members Diana Vines and Tammy Williams, who had both played for DePaul University and the WBA's Indiana Stars. Community leaders and women's basketball supporters also joined the crowd.

The Twisters' head coach was Stephanie Tamayo-Rivera, wife of NFL Coach of the Year Ron Rivera, a former Chicago Bears linebacker. The team picked up Natalie Perrino (also from DePaul and the Indiana Stars). They later added Staci Carney from Purdue University, E.C. Hill and Cindy Conner from Northern Illinois University, and Maureen "Mo" Holahan, who was All-Big Ten at Northwestern University. After that the Twisters recruited players from all over Illinois.

In 1995, the Naismith Basketball Hall of Fame in Springfield, Massachusetts, honored Kandi Conda as the first African-American woman to manage a women's professional basketball team. In 2014 the African-American Hall of Fame awarded her its "Athletics Award" for her "outstanding commitment to the community and the world."

The team practiced at some "swanky" gyms, and Alumni Hall at DePaul University hosted the Twisters's home games.

But the reorganization and franchise deposit would not be enough to sustain the 1995 season. I asked again. "Lord, I really got to know what you want me to do. I'm really struggling. I know you've been with me all along. I think I need a TV deal. On the other hand, I don't know how to get this done."

...

After that, an idea popped into my mind: contact a sports network. I thought if we could get an all-star game televised, revenues might solve our problem. So I called the sports directors at the local TV stations asking if they knew how I could contact ESPN. I called the sports network, but they weren't interested. Then I called the CEOs of NBC, ABC, and CBS. Of course, I didn't reach the CEOs, but the operators connected me with the persons who led sports programming. They all pushed me out. None of them had heard of me or the WBA. The sports programmers didn't think there would be interest in us. They all turned me down.

Later on, my brother Joe Lee Mitchell (the same brother who lent me his American Express card for the exhibition tour) knew what I was doing. He'd heard of a new network. "Why don't you try Sports Channel America?" he asked. "It's a new sports network looking for new ideas." I called information in Dallas, but the operator could find no listings for Sports Channel America.

A friend named Dewart Cummings and his family were staunch supporters when the WBA had a team in Beatrice, Nebraska. Dewart told me about a story he'd seen on CNN, the cable news network, about a 24-hour women's sports and entertainment network through Prime Sports. He also said he thought he'd seen an article about Prime Sports in the New York *Times*. I

The Vision

called the *Times,* and a reporter FAXed me a copy of the article and gave me the phone number of Prime Sports in Dallas.

I called Prime Sports and talked to a program manager named Chris Manual. He asked me to send him a package of information so he could look it over during the weekend. He said he'd call me the following Monday. He failed to return my call. On Tuesday, I called again.

"I'm sorry, he's on vacation," the receptionist said.

"May I talk with someone else," I asked, "preferably Chris's supervisor."

Lynne Heddow came on the line. After I explained what I wanted, she looked in Chris's office. "I can't find the information. Will you send it to me again?"

She asked me to send her a video so she could see the level of play. I had a nice highlight video to send her. I put together a package that also included brochures and flyers about the league and overnighted it to her. On Friday, I called to confirm that she had the materials.

"I'm overwhelmed by the quality of the players," she said. "I might have something here I can put on the air. Give me the weekend to look it over. I'll call you on Monday."

On Monday, with no call from Lynne, I called back.

"Lynne has the day off," the receptionist said. "She'll be back tomorrow."

I called again on Tuesday, only to find she still had not returned.

"What?" I hung up, feeling anger and frustration. I stewed about it for a few days. On Thursday, I decided to call Lynne's boss. Unfortunately, I had misplaced the Prime Sports phone number.

That's when God connected me with Liberty Sports of Dallas, Texas.

The information operator said she had no listing for Prime Sports, but she knew of a Dallas company called Liberty Sports that owned a lot of sports networks. With nothing to lose, I asked for the number, and she connected me. When the receptionist answered, I was still fuming. All I could think of was Lynne's first name.

"Let me speak to Lynne," I said.

After being connected to two more receptionists, I got connected. I ran off at the mouth barely containing my anger. I spouted off about how the WBA could be an asset to their network and how upset I was that I had twice been promised a call back and twice not gotten a return call.

"Whoa! Whoa! Whoa!" a man said. "You must mean Lynne from our Houston branch."

That's when I realized I was talking to a man – not the woman I had talked to before.

"I'm so sorry," I said. "I've got the wrong Lynne?"

His name was Lynn Geick. "Actually, I like what I'm hearing," he said. "Why don't you mail me copies of what you sent to her?"

I figured what the heck. I'd already made a fool of myself. At least I could do that. It would only cost me another $11.95 to overnight it. The next day I called to

The Vision

see if he'd received the information.

"I'd like to fly to Kansas City to meet with you," Lynn said. "What's your schedule on Tuesday?"

I still had no idea who he was, but I thought this might be important. Now, I never had a schedule. I just went with the flow of things. But I grabbed a writing pad and started pushing papers around so it would sound like I was looking at my schedule. Of course, all the pages were blank. "Tuesday looks fine."

"I'll fly into Kansas City International."

"I'll pick you up."

On Tuesday, I met Lynn Geick and Fred D. McCallister, at the airport. Lynn turned out to be the senior vice president of development for Liberty Sports. Fred was vice president and associate general counsel. Liberty owned a group of formerly regional sports networks – including Sports Channel America – that broadcast regional sports events, including professional, collegiate, and high school teams, usually limited to each network's market area.

In 1994 Liberty brought them all under the name Prime Sports. With the new brand, the individual networks shifted toward a common programming schedule, adding sporting events from other regions. They were also planning to start a Woman's Sports Network in January 1995. (Two years later Prime Sports networks became part of the Fox Sports Net with such regional networks as Fox Sports Midwest.)

Debbie Summers met us at the KC Masterpiece restaurant on Kansas City's Country Club Plaza for some authentic Kansas City barbecue. After we ate, Lynn said, "I'd like to meet your staff."

I took them to my apartment. I was working from home, because that was the only place I had to work from.

"It's great that you bring your work home with you," Lynn said. "But I want to meet the rest of your staff."

"Well you met Debbie," I said. "Her husband Pee Wee Summers is at work at their State Farm insurance agency. That's the staff."

They said they were under the impression that we had a hundred employees in a big building somewhere downtown. "How can you run an eight-state program from here?"

I smiled. "It's all by the grace of God."

"We want in," Lynn said. "Does the league have any debts?"

"Yes. About $220,000."

"Bring us records of the debt."

I did, and they wrote checks to cover them right there in my apartment. Before they left, we were partners in this venture. Liberty became an investor with forty-nine percent ownership interest. I became the WBA's founder and director of operations.

They agreed to televise all of the 1995 WBA regular season, all-star, and playoff games on Prime Sports networks. Our games were part of three hundred women's sporting events the organization would broadcast that year. It seemed my prayers had been answered.

Liberty Sports brought along some capable staff to help make the WBA successful. Already mentioned were Lynn Geick and Fred McCallister. Lynn Geick had fourteen years experience in communications and nineteen years in finance. In addition to his role developing new business ventures, he also acted as the general manager of Prime Sports Radio.

Fred McCallister's administrative duties included managing all league operations. Previously he had also been associate general counsel for Prime Sports West in Los Angeles, California.

Mark Faber was vice president of league marketing. He had spent five years with the NFL's Dallas Cowboys, where he served as assistant vice president of marketing and vice president of training camp marketing. He had also worked in television sales and syndication. For the WBA, he developed marketing strategies and corporate partnership programs.

The Liberty team also included Mike Harter, who served as team liason. He had experience in sports and entertainment with the Meadowlands and Monmouth Park Racetracks in New Jersey, and the Tucson Toros, the AAA affiliate for the Houston Astros, and Prime Network. Judy Dunn was administrative assistant. She arranged daily business activities for the WBA, as well as helping league offices across the country and assisting Lynn Geick.

Even though I was delighted that Liberty Sports came on board, not everyone was happy about it.

"I found out that Liberty Sports had purchased the

entire league, except for two of the teams," said Kandi Conda in *It's Your Go Season*. "I'm still not sure how all of this happened ... I was very distraught to find out that I would no longer own the team."

Kandi understood that the sale was the only way we could get television coverage. She stayed on to manage the Twisters. "It was about making the league better for women and keeping my promise to them," she said. "So I put my personal pride aside and stayed on as director of operations and general manager."

Unfortunately, because of league finances she never got a refund on her franchise deposit. All owners were required to pay the entire $28,000 up front. But the league made a small exception for Kandi. The remaining $18,000 had not been paid before Liberty bought in.

...

We took a look at the Greater Kansas City area and decided that having the Kansas City Mustangs and the Kansas Marauders in the same area was more or less taking away a powerful program in the league. We had a lot of good players on that Kansas squad, and point guard Geri "Kay Kay" Hart, who'd earned All-America honors at the University of Kansas, was one of the best.

We talked about moving the Kansas Marauders to Wichita. And we had an interested investor. However, we played an exhibition game there, and fan support just wasn't there. Instead, that franchise moved to Louisville to become the Kentucky Marauders.

When we moved that team to Kentucky, we moved some of the Kansas players to the Kansas City

The Vision

Mustangs. Debbie Summers, Harvey Randall, and Calvin Thompson came on as the Mustangs' coaches. And Joe C. Meriweather and Jamie Collins came on board later in the season. Other Kansas players moved to the St. Louis RiverQueens. However, Kay Kay Hart decided to pursue her medical degree and left the organization.

...

The 1995 WBA home opener on April 15 saw the Chicago Twisters defeat the Kentucky Marauders 135-105. The Twisters featured two Chicago players who had been Chicago *Sun-Times* Players of the Year. Jennifer Jones, who played college ball at Kansas State University, won the honor in 1983, and E.C. Hill won in 1990. She later played at Northern Illinois University. Diana Vines, who led scoring in the opener with 39 points, was a Chicago high school teacher and basketball coach. Other local stars included another Northern Illinois Huskie Cindy Connor, as well as a former Loyola University Chicago standout Stacy Kundinger, and two players with ties to DePaul University: Natalie Perrino, who played there, and DePaul's assistant basketball coach Staci Carney.

"The talent is incredible," Twisters Coach Stephanie Tamayo-Rivera told the *Sun-Times*. "It's almost like having an all-star team from Chicago."

Besides that, operations were going well. "The league is more organized this year," Diana Vines of the Twisters told the *Sun-Times*. "It's being run on a much more professional level all around the league."

1995 WBA Rosters

Chicago Twisters

Head Coach: Stephanie Tamayo-Rivera
Assistant Coach: Michael Moseley
Team Assistant: George Washington
Director of Operations and Manager: Kandi Conda

Lori Bakhaus	McKendree College
Staci Carney	Purdue University
Cindy Connor	Northern Illinois University
Nadine Galindo	University of North Dakota
E.C. Hill	Northern Illinois University
Maureen "Mo" Holahan	Northwestern University
Jennifer Jones	Kansas State University
Stacy Kundinger	Loyola University Chicago
Natalie Perrino	DePaul University
Bolivia Thompson	Long Beach State University
Diana Vines	DePaul University
Acquanetta Washington	University of Illinois
Tammy Williams	DePaul University

1995 WBA Rosters (continued)

Kansas City Mustangs
Head Coach: Joe C. Meriweather
Assistant Coach: Jamie Collins
Trainer: Joe Morgan, Jr.

Lisa Braddy	University of Kansas
Shawna Brown	Missouri Western State University
Sarah Campbell	University of Missouri
Joy Champ	Pittsburg State University
Latrice Ervin	Mid-America Nazarene College
Lashon Gant	Avila University
Robelyn Garcia	University of Nebraska
Ceci Harris	University of Colorado
Evette Ott	University of Kansas
Lisa Tate	University of Kansas
Lashawne Thomas	University of Missouri at Kansas City
Melissa Ulsaker	Emporia State University
Stephanie Worthy	University of Missouri at Kansas City

1995 WBA Rosters (continued)

Kentucky Marauders
Head Coach: Carl Harvey, Jr.
Operations Manager: Shedrick J. Jones, Sr.

Krista Blunk	University of Evansville
Michelle Clark	Western Kentucky University
Tracye Davis	University of Kentucky
Kim Hartley	Eastern Kentucky University
Patty Jo Hedges-Ward	University of Kentucky
Denise Hill	Western Kentucky University
Christe Jordan	University of Kentucky
Leslie Nichols	University of Kentucky
Jennifer O'Bryan	Bellamarine College
Joyce Price	Indiana University
Lea Robinson	Western Kentucky University
Leatrice Scott	University of Louisiana
Nova Sweet	University of Louisiana
Renee Westmoreland	Western Kentucky University

1995 WBA Rosters (continued)

Memphis Blues
Head Coach: Wanda Jones
Assistant Coaches: Gary Meyers, Alvin Abston

Carolyn Blair	Shelby State University/ Knoxville College
Audrey Covington	Memphis State University
Sarina Crawford	Mississippi Valley State University
Lori Davis	Shelby State University
Terri Donald	University of Alabama
Ronda Lauderdale	Memphis State University
Andrea Martre	Shelby State University
Beverly Pryor	Shelby State University
Pamela Scaife	Delta State University
Crystal Smith	Delta State University
Priscilla Sweeney	Kansas State University
Angeline Ward	Memphis State University

1995 WBA Rosters (continued)

Minnesota Stars
Head Coach: Chris Hester
Operations Manager: Tony Queen

Dee Dee Deeken	University of Illinois
Crystal Flint	University of Minnesota
Ellen Hebert	University of Minnesota
Sarah Howard	St. Cloud State University
Mary Klotzbeecher	University of Minnesota
Kathy Mobely	St. Cloud State University
Jan Niehaus	St. Cloud State University
Veronica Rutter	Oral Roberts University
Kelly Skalicky	Louisiana State University
Molly Tadich	University of Minnesota
Queen Wilson	St. Cloud State University

1995 WBA Rosters (continued)

Nebraska Xpress
Head Coach: Scott Long

Lisa Carlsen	Northwest Missouri State University
Julie Dale	Southern Connecticut State University
Renee Dozier	University of Missouri
Maurtice Ivy	University of Nebraska
Kelly Luenenberg	University of Nebraska at Omaha
Tynetta Rasheed	Iowa State University
Melissa Sanford	Creighton University
Sandy Skrodski	University of Nebraska at Omaha
Shannon Struby	Creighton University
Rissa Taylor	University of Nebraska
Meggan Yedjena	University of Nebraska

1995 WBA Rosters (continued)

Oklahoma Flames
Head Coach: Jamie Collins
Operations Manager: Richard McGonagle

Ketra Bell	Bartlesville Wesleyan
Tatya Brown-Glascoe	Louisiana Tech University
Marla Duncan	Oklahoma University
Cledella Evans	Iowa State University
LaRon Fowler	Johnson County Community College
Helen Garrett	Oral Roberts University
Larissa Gritts	Phillips University
Stephanie Hadley	Northeastern University
Lisa Kirby	Oklahoma City University
Lisa Long	University of Iowa
Patrice Marshall	Bartlesville Wesleyan
Jo Mosley	Oklahoma University
Lynn Page	University of Kansas

1995 WBA Rosters (continued)

St. Louis RiverQueens
Head coach: Randy Kriewall
Operations manager: Bill Hanks
General Managers: Margo and Paul Garvin

Chris Aldridge	Eastern Illinois State University
Renee Bishop	Southwest Missouri State University
Karen Herman	Washington State University
Petra Jackson	Southern Illinois University
Kim McClelland	University of Illinois
Kim Rolfing	Drake University
Lisa Sandbothe	University of Missouri
Mary Helen Walker	Holy Cross
Susan Wellman	Illinois State University

Before the 1995 season players sometimes had to drive long distances to games in rental vans. They'd also been promised $50 per game. Sometimes they didn't get that.

Still, I think the players knew that they could trust me in what I was trying to do for them. They also knew that, as the founder of the league, I would do anything for them, even if it meant giving them the last dollar that I had in my pocket or going without a meal myself. Somehow I felt they knew me better than I knew myself. I remember times when we were really struggling, wondering whether we could pay for meals or motel bills because we didn't have a good crowd that night. A lot of the players would say, "Don't worry about paying us this week. Just take care of the bills. We're with you."

Once Liberty Sports bought the league, players got $100 per game, plus travel, food, and minor expenses. Coaches and managers also got small payments. The teams could reserve vans for trips to nearby venues. And they flew to games farther than fifty miles away. It was what I had dreamed of at the tryouts in 1992 when I told the new players they wouldn't be traveling first class.

But even that posed a bit of a problem for the Twisters. Kandi Conda told one such story in *It's Your Go Season!* Even though Kandi had instituted a policy that the team had to wear dress clothes on flights, one of the players showed up at O'Hare International Airport

The Vision

wearing shorts and flip flops.

"Where are your required dress clothes?" Kandi asked.

"I'm not wearing them," the player said.

"You can't get on the plane without dress clothes. I'm going to leave you here in Chicago."

"You won't leave me. You need me to win."

"Well, I guess we'll have to see if we can win without you."

Kandi left her in the airport, and the rest of the players refused to speak to her for the entire flight.

"They played their hearts out and won the game," Kandi said. "They were excited and learned that they could do it without her, and she never ignored the rules again."

Later, after Kandi's tough love showed that she meant business, she and the player became close friends.

During the 1995 season, some teams experienced trouble among teammates. They formed cliques and had hotel roommate conflicts and personal issues. For the Chicago Twisters, it became too much for the coach to handle.

"The coach threatened to leave if I didn't come in to assist," Kandi said in *It's Your Go Season!* "After that, I traveled along with her and the team to every one of the away games."

...

Some of the WBA players were kind of cocky, but the point is they were that good. Still, they respected the other players, even those with lessor skills. They were always team players. "I respected every individual for what she brought," said Petra Jackson of the St. Louis RiverQueens. "We didn't hang out after games. Nor were some of us friends, but that didn't matter. We played for a common goal, and that was to win a championship. We knew who to get the ball to and when. We had several people who consistently averaged double figures, and it didn't matter as long as we got the 'W.' We made each other better."

A sense of camaraderie existed among all the players, no matter which teams they played for. "After the game, whether we won or lost, we respected each other as women and athletes. The home team played hostesses, and we had great times off the court, as well as on."

...

One of the WBA stars that season was Robbie Garcia. She'd been with us from the beginning on the 1992 touring exhibition team. In 1993 she was an All-Star on the first championship team, the Kansas Crusaders. The next year she moved to the Kansas City Mustangs. Again, she was an All-Star on the undefeated regular season team. Robbie played only half of the 1995 season. A total of nine knee surgeries took their toll. She retired as a player and moved in to the Mustangs front office as player personnel director. She also did radio announcing for the entire league. She made a short comeback at the end of the 1995 season to play for her championship coach Jamie Collins with the Oklahoma Flames in Tulsa.

...

1995 WBA Regular Season Results

American Conference:

Team	Win/Loss Record
Chicago Twisters	15-1
Nebraska Xpress	6-9
Minnesota Stars	5-10
Oklahoma Flames	5-10

National Conference:

Team	Win/Loss Record
St. Louis RiverQueens	9-7
Kansas City Mustangs	7-8
Kentucky Marauders	7-8
Memphis Blues	7-8

...

The 1995 WBA All-Star game, held May 27 at Municipal Auditorium in Kansas City, Missouri, pitted the best of the National Conference against the stars from the American Conference. The three-year-old Kansas City Mustangs of the Nationals hosted the game. The announced attendance was 3,426, and the game was televised by Prime Sports. The National Conference won the game 89-67.

From the tip-off on, the players ran hard and played strong defense. For the whole game they were running and shooting and running and passing and running and scoring. They ran, ran, ran. Hard.

"The coach told us to get in and run and have fun," said guard Laurie Byrd of the Kentucky Marauders, as reported in the Kansas City *Star*. "She put in our fast squad, and we ran the break real well. We were the home team, and the crowd got into the game, and that helped."

At half-time, the American team, coached by Stephanie Tamayo-Rivera of the Chicago Twisters, led 45-37. They held the lead through the third quarter, when the Nationals exploded. At one point the Americans missed eleven shots in a row, while Laurie Byrd made four shots in a row, and forward Ronda Lauderdale of the Memphis Blues dropped two successive three-pointers. The Nationals outscored the opponents 36-8 in the fourth quarter to win 89-76.

Nationals Coach Jean Pate of the St. Louis RiverQueens credited her team's speed and quickness for the win. "I was trying to get everybody six minutes a quarter," she told the Kansas City *Star*. "The timing rotation worked out just right. But the way we were going, I wasn't going to change back with the speed and quickness we had going."

Ronda Lauderdale, who scored 18 points, won Most Valuable Player honors. Renee Dozier of Nebraska was the leading scorer for the Americans with 13 points.

Geri "Kay-Kay" Hart, an All-America selection from the University of Kansas, and Robbie Garcia, who had played at the University of Nebraska and the WBA's

The Vision

Kansas Crusaders, Kansas City Mustangs, and Oklahoma Flames announced the game on Fox Radio. And, as promised, Prime Sports aired the game on both coasts, as well as in the Midwest. Nancy "Lady Magic" Lieberman, a powerhouse from Old Dominion University in Virginia, was the TV announcer.

...

1995 National Conference All-Stars

Chris Aldridge	St. Louis RiverQueens
Carolyn Blair	Memphis Blues
Lisa Braddy	Kansas City Mustangs
Laurie Byrd	Kentucky Marauders
Terri Donald	Memphis Blues
Patty Jo Edges-Ward	Kentucky Marauders
Petra Jackson	St. Louis RiverQueens
Ronda Lauderdale	Memphis Blues
Evette Ott	Kansas City Mustangs
Danielle Shareef	St. Louis RiverQueens
Lisa Tate	Kansas City Mustangs

1995 American Conference All-Stars

Lisa Carlsen	Nebraska Xpress
Cindy Connor	Chicago Twisters
Dee Dee Deeken	Minnesota Stars
Renee Dozier	Nebraska Xpress
Helen Garrett	Oklahoma Flames
Jo Mosley	Oklahoma Flames
Jan Niehaus	Minnesota Stars
Lynn Page	Oklahoma Flames
Melissa Sanford	Nebraska Xpress
Molly Tadich	Minnesota Stars
Diana Vines	Chicago Twisters
Tammy Williams	Chicago Twisters

...

We had planned to run another championship tournament at the end of the 1995 season, with playoffs leading to a championship series. In fact, the Kansas City Mustangs had just earned a playoff berth a week before the July playoffs were set to start by defeating the Memphis Blues 100-96 at Kansas City's Municipal Auditorium. Attendance had been 613, so we were starting to fill the seats at regular season games.

The Kansas City team came out slow. Only their twelve first-quarter free throws kept them in the game. By half-time, though, the Blues led 53-41 behind players Angiline Ward, and Terri Donald who each scored 16 in the game and Ronda Lauderdale with 14.

The Vision

Other Blues players included Lori Davis, Brenda Hatchet, Priscilla Sweeney, and Andrea Marte,

In the locker room, the Kansas players got serious. "We ended up saying we need to dig deep and find your heart," Stacy Truitt told the Kansas City *Star*. "I think we got a little more relaxed."

Basketball lore has it that you can often tell which team is going to win a game by watching the first five minutes of the second half. That held true in this game. The Mustangs came back with a vengeance, outscoring the Blues 23-5 in the first 6:30 of the third quarter behind Sarah Campbell, who scored 10 points in three minutes.

Leading scorer for the Mustangs was Evette Ott with 23 points. Stacy Truitt had 21 points and 11 rebounds for a double-double, followed by Lisa Tate with another double-double with 17 points and 11 rebounds, along with four steals and three blocked shots. Also playing for the Mustangs were Stephanie Jones, Amy Fordham, LaShawne Thomas, and Joy Champ.

But the real difference came on the defensive end of the court. The Mustangs' full-court press forced seven Blues's turnovers.

"If we play defense like we're capable of, we get a lot of easy baskets," Mustangs Coach Calvin Thompson told the Kansas City *Star*. "That was the key."

As the game clock wound down, things got crazy. Kansas City threw the ball away four times, but Memphis couldn't take advantage. They missed six of their last seven shots. We didn't know it then, but the game turned out to be one of the WBA's last regular season games.

...

We all wanted to hold the entire playoff and championship tournament, but we also wanted to conserve funds for the next year. A week before we were supposed to start the playoffs, the league cancelled its six-team system. The Chicago Twisters and the St. Louis RiverQueens had won their conferences. So we held one championship game between them. The RiverQueens were 9-6 in regular season, having lost twice to the Twisters. The Twisters entered the tournament with a 14-1 record.

As the WBA teams prepared for the championship series, the American Basketball League (ABL) announced its plan to start a women's league in the fall of 1996, working from a league office in Palo Alto, California. But our players had a game to prepare for. The championship game was held at the University of Missouri-St. Louis and drew about 1,000 fans.

Petra Jackson scored six of the RiverQueens' 10 points off the tip to give her team a 10-7 lead. The Twisters came back and tied the game at 12-12. The Twisters then opened a 22-17 lead by the end of the first quarter.

"We were prepared for their adjustments," Twisters Coach Stephanie Tamayo-Rivera told the *St. Louis Post-Dispatch*. "Even though we were prepared, we made some mistakes. But we stayed calm and got back into our offense."

The Vision

By half-time Chicago led 43-34, due in part to the RiverQueens' 15 turnovers. "We only had a couple more turnovers than they did," St. Louis coach Jean Pate told the *Post-Dispatch*. "But ours were caused more by not running our offense."

In the second half the Twisters pulled ahead 58-41, but the RiverQueens never gave up. They kept chipping away at the lead. "We weren't going to give up, but we couldn't get the ball to fall for us," Jean continued. "Every time we cut the lead to six points, they'd run away again."

By the final minutes, however, St. Louis was still in a position to win. With 2:28 left in the game, the RiverQueens pulled within six points 97-91, thanks in part to three technical fouls called on the Twisters in a two-minute period. Jackson made all six free throws to give her team some hope. The trouble was that for every basket St. Louis scored, Chicago answered.

"They scored every time we didn't need them to," Jackson told the *Post-Dispatch* after the game. "They came through in the clutch."

The RiverQueens had only four substitutes during the game, and all but 15 of their points came from four players. Petra Jackson ended the game with game-high 32 points. "I was hotter than a firecracker," she said, recalling the game twenty years later.

Post player Danielle Shareef had 24 points. Sarita Wesley scored 16, and Renee Bishop sank 10. By contrast, the Twisters had even scoring all the way down their bench. Diana Vines scored 31 points. The rest came from eight other Chicago players.

"They were putting it to us," Petra Jackson of the RiverQueens said. "but we came back on them and got within 1 point.

But the Twisters won 107-96, with Diana Vines and Petra Jackson named co-MVPs.

"My hopes of winning my ring was shattered," Petra said.

Reporters from *Sports Illustrated* and other major media outlets covered the game. And *Sports Illustrated for Kids* ran an article about it. It seemed like we were finally getting somewhere. But rumors continued.

"After the championship game, we walked around for six months awaiting our fate," said Twisters manager Kandi Conda said in *It's Your Go Season!* "We all thought that something big was about to happen. We heard that we would possibly be purchased by the NBA or that Liberty Sports would expand us."

The worst was yet to come.

Chapter 9
Air Ball

Soon more news of the American Basketball League (ABL) hit the media. The University of Kansas women's basketball coach, Marian Washington, served on the ABL's advisory board. She, too, saw the potential for professional basketball for women. "There're such proven female athletes that if there's strong marketing and promotion, there'll be a great chance of being successful," she told the Kansas City *Star* at the time.

The ABL's start-up funding was $4 million according to the *Star*. They were selling franchises for $3 million each. But they still had to pay for staff, transportation, advertising, and arena rentals. The new league reportedly promised players average annual salaries of $70,000. But they asked players for "agreements" instead of formal contracts. They planned to play from October to February. That pitted them against the men's NBA and the men's and women's NCAA teams for basketball fans.

I wasn't worried about the ABL. I didn't see how

they could survive unless they could come up with $24 million by February 1996. There wasn't yet enough demand for the kind of money they were throwing around out there. I was confident that they couldn't last two years at that rate.

By contrast, Liberty Sports had more modest expenses, and they planned to broadcast 100 WBA games over three years on its Prime Network. They also planned to pay staff and players full-time salaries for the summer 1996 season.

I highly doubted that both leagues would exist in 1996. I could have guaranteed that there would be only one.

…

Plans for the 1996 season took off. We planned to expand. Robbie Garcia and a friend planned to buy a new WBA franchise that would play at the Johnson County Community College in Overland Park, Kansas. Robbie would serve as owner and general manager.

I looked forward to a successful 1996 season. Liberty Sports officials decided they wanted to bring all the WBA teams under one umbrella to have full control of the league. That meant we'd have to buy back the Kansas City and St. Louis franchises. Liberty Sports would then control the entire league, but the franchise owners would no longer have to worry about the kinds of financial issues they had both encountered. Liberty Sports offered both owners four times their investments, plus a percentage of the profits as long as the league existed. While Liberty Sports was negotiating

The Vision

with the owners, the league told Kandi Conda, who had made a deposit for the Chicago Twisters franchise, that if the deal went through, she'd get her deposit back.

Ron, the Kansas City Mustangs owner, agreed. He also encouraged Margo Garvin, the St. Louis RiverQueens owner, to sell. But Margo blocked the shot. She wanted more than Liberty Sports offered, and she wasn't going to sell unless she got it. Liberty Sports, being all about business, refused.

"We offered her a fair deal," said Lynn Geick, the Liberty Sports vice president who made the original deal with me. "We really wanted this to work." He told me not to worry about the close to a quarter-million dollars in WBA debt they had paid off. With that, Liberty Sports walked away.

I didn't know which direction to go, but I was trying to come up with some ideas. We'd been going so well. Liberty Sports had done such a great job showing us the potential of the league. At the WBA All-Star game, we seated more than three thousand fans for the first time. And the game was televised nationwide. Now all this was lost. I began to look for other sources of financial support for survival.

We'd come through difficulties before, and I'd always kept the faith. I never was one to give up, because you never know what's still around the corner. I couldn't quit.

...

Then came the news of the NBA's new professional women's basketball league.

The WBA folded soon after that. The loss affected everyone affiliated with the league. The WNBA adopted many of the WBA's rules and practices – including a spring/summer season as opposed to winter when basketball was traditionally played. They even started teams in four cities where we already had teams.

"We were all devastated and trying to navigate our way through the women's pro basketball puzzle," Kandi Conda said in *It's Your Go Season!*

At the same time, though, I was somehow thankful for what God had allowed us to accomplish. And I knew that the WNBA could take women's professional basketball to its next level.

"The WBA was the beginning for the ABL and the WNBA," said Petra Jackson of the St. Louis RiverQueens. "It was a feeling of self-fulfillment. Lightning had a vision, and he did whatever he could to keep that vision to give us an opportunity to continue our dream of playing basketball. And to this day, the WBA players have a bond of belonging to one of the teams of the 1990s, and no one can take away what Lightning did for us. I thank him and Margo Gavin for making it happen for us in St. Louis."

The ABL launched in the fall of 1996 and played another season in 1997. They began a new season in November 1998, but they were plagued by the same financial issues that the WBA dealt with. They ran out of money and ceased operations on December 22, 1998.

Some of our players, in particular the RiverQueen's Charmin Smith and Chicago Twisters' starting guard

The Vision

E.C. Hill, but maybe others as well, later played with the ABL. Both also went to the WNBA. Charmin Smith played three years with WNBA's Minnesota Lynx, Seattle Storm, and Phoenix Mercury. E.C. Hill played four years with WNBA's Charlotte Sting in 2000, Phoenix Mercury and Los Angeles Sparks in 2001, and Orlando Miracle in 2002.

As the WNBA teams took the court in 1997, I expected some sort of recognition for paving the way for the new professional league. None came. In fact, a decade later when the WNBA celebrated its tenth anniversary, its Web site mentioned the ABL, but not a word about the WBA.

In an interview with Val Ackerman, entitled "Val Ackerman Celebrates Ten Years of the WNBA" Val answered the question "Were you ever afraid that the (WNBA) might grow too fast or get a little too big for itself?"

Her answer included, "... at the time the (WNBA) started, there was another league, the ABL, which was just getting started ..."

The WBA was in existence at the time, and we had just come off our biggest All-Star game ever. But, there was no mention of the league in the article.

Record-Setting All-Star Game

Chapter 10
Overtime

I went into restaurant management with Golden Corral. I know that's where God wanted me, because that's where I met my wife Sandra Mitchell. One day around the end of June I looked up as the place was about to open, and she was standing first in line. I knew right then that she was supposed to be in my life. I also knew that if she left the restaurant that day and I hadn't talked to her, I'd never see her again. I did talk to her that day, and we married five months later.

As time went on I often thought about the WBA. The part that bothered me most was the players never got the recognition they deserved. God wouldn't let me walk away. I decided I wanted to tell their story. I wanted them to be acknowledged and to tell people that it all happened through the grace of God. I couldn't let it go. I thought that once the story was told, that would be the final chapter.

In May 2007 I sent my wife, Sandra Mitchell, and my daughter Angela McFarquhar to the library to look for information on the WBA.

When they got home Angela handed me an article they had found. "Dad, you need to see this."

The article was about the WNBA written by Roth Talent Associates the year before. It mentioned Val Ackerman and identified her as the "founder and former president" of the WNBA from 1997 to 2005. It jumped out at me from the printed page. Val Ackerman – the same woman I'd talked to about sponsoring the WBA – was the founder and first president of the WNBA.

I couldn't believe it. I had never seen any mentions of her connections with the WNBA until then. And also from reading the article, I learned for the first time that she was a staff attorney for the NBA and assistant to Commissioner David Stern. I had put my trust in her. I shared my dream and my hopes. When I found out that she was the one who created the WNBA, it was like someone stabbed me.

...

The NBA and WNBA had caused me severe pain by stealing my dream. Reading this article brought it all up to me again. I decided to sue them for infliction of mental distress. By then I had changed jobs and was working at the Hometown Buffet six days a week and feeling angry about no one recognizing the WBA. During my one day off each week, I spend as much time as I could in prayer about a lawsuit against the WNBA.

In January 2008 I looked for an attorney to handle this for me. Some even charged me just to talk to them. Almost every firm I contacted said the case would be a conflict of interest for their practice. Ones who would handle the case needed thousands of dollars up front. I didn't have that kind of money. So it came down to my fighting the NBA and WNBA on my own with God's help or forgetting anything ever happened. Knowing I couldn't forget it, my wife, Sandy, and I looked for other sources of help.

I called the law library at the University of Missouri at Kansas City. "Is it possible for me to come into the library for research even if I don't go to school there?"

The librarian said yes, so my family and I went there to look for any information to help prepare the papers for the court. A librarian there explained how we could proceed, using library materials. Books we found there helped us prepare all the paperwork for the case. We did a lot of legwork, and I worked on the information late into the night. When I did go to bed, I spent many restless nights lying awake, or getting up to write down stuff that would be helpful.

Once Sandy and I felt we had gathered enough information for the case, we put it together to present to the clerk of the court. When we were ready, we drove to the federal courthouse in Kansas City, Missouri. I was pretty nervous even about going into the courthouse to file the suit. When we arrived, a parking place was hard to find. We made three or four trips around the courthouse, and each trip added to the pounding on my nerves.

Finally, we went in and told a clerk we wanted to file a lawsuit. She gave us the form to use, and we started filling it out. That was no easy task. There were things on the form we didn't understand. I went back and forth and back and forth to the window to be sure we filled out the paperwork the right way. When I handed it to the clerk, she asked for the filing fee. I think it was $300.

We didn't have a lot of money, but Sandy knew how important this was to me. "If you file the suit, I think you'll get some relief," she said. "You might even get to the point where you can watch women's basketball again."

I hadn't wanted to watch any women's games because of the sour taste it gave me, reminding me that it seemed like everything I'd done for the WBA had been all for nothing. I was determined for that not to be so for everyone else associated with the WBA.

My wife and I agreed to go ahead and file.

However, the case cost more than we had figured it would. In addition to the filing fee, we paid extra for the papers to be delivered to the NBA. And we spent extra money for making copies and buying gasoline to drive to the courthouse, plus parking fees when we got there. We neglected a few bills to do all this, and that eventually caused some serious issues. But still we wanted to pursue it.

To determine the amount I would sue for, I decided to set it much higher than I expected and high enough to get their attention. Representing myself, I filed suit in federal court seeking $500 million. The court action was covered in an article posted on *Missouri Lawyers Media.com,* which covers legal news, court opinions, verdicts and settlements, foreclosures, and public notices in Missouri.

By the grace of God, what we prepared was enough for the judge to set up mediation between the two parties to the suit. We thought that if we could get to the mediation, we had a shot. But waiting was the hard part. The sense of not knowing what would happen or even when it would happen caused tension in our household.

While we waited for the mediation, my wife got hurt on the job. She was paralyzed on one side of her body and could no longer help me with my research. In fact, I had to help her with such ordinary activities as showering and combing her hair. Her condition required things we didn't have money for. We lost one of our cars. That didn't really matter, because without her working we needed only one. But it added another sense of loss to the feeling of loss I had from ceasing operation of the WBA.

Also during that time, having lost my wife's income, we had to give up our home and move into an apartment. Sometimes when I looked at my wife, I saw the worries. I really wanted to quit, but she wouldn't let me. She understood how losing the WBA hurt me when it happened. She understood more than I did.

Things around the house felt pretty dim, because we were going through so much. More tragedies befell us. My mother, Ollie Mae, father Ned Sr., and brother Billy E. Mitchell all died within about a year and a half. And one of my daughters had marital troubles, so two of our grandsons came to live with us.

Through it all, though, by the grace of God we kept our hope. We never gave up our trust in God. We knew that someway, somehow God was going to bring us through it. We wouldn't stop. We believed in what we were trying to accomplish.

...

Unfortunately, the result of the court case was a huge disappointment. The other side pointed out that I had gone past the statute of limitations to file the suit. The statute of limitations was five years from the date that the events took place. We shut down the WBA in 1995, and the WNBA opened in 1996. I had only until 2001 to take my case to court. My suit was thrown out on the technicality (time barred), which simply means my time had run out – right or wrong.

My brother Joe Lee and I went into the Johnson County court in Kansas and tried to file a case there. We couldn't, though, because the federal case had already been dismissed. I had to accept the fact that getting relief in the courts was not going to happen.

...

Finally, it became clear that God had other plans for professional women's basketball in the United States. And, of course, God has the last say. I know the Lord is in control, and I'm always ready and willing to be an instrument in His hands.

And I'm proud of what we accomplished and what it meant to people. I'm happy to tell the story so the players, coaches, and staff of the WBA are finally

The Vision

recognized.

Most of all, I'm happy for what the WBA did for our players. As Robbie Garcia, of the Kansas Crusaders and the Kansas City Mustangs, said, "The WBA gave me the opportunity to live a lifelong dream of continuing my basketball career after college. The WBA and basketball as a whole positively impacted my self-esteem, self-confidence, and sense of accomplishment."

Diana Vines of the WBA's Iowa Unicorns, Indiana Stars, and Chicago Twisters echoed Petra's sentiment. "The WBA gave me a sense of purpose – a sense of success and completeness. Playing and winning a championship were things that I dreamed of as a little girl – and being able to do that in the United States as a professional athlete. The journey itself was amazing. The competition was the best of any competition out here today."

Our players showed that a women's league was possible and that there was an audience for it. Many women's professional basketball leagues have come and gone, but no one could find the right formula to succeed. But God, by His grace, gave me a vision to create the WBA with a foundation that showed that women's professional basketball was possible by creating a spring and summer league. And with that American women share the same opportunity their male counterparts have had for decades: to play professional basketball here at home before family, relatives, and friends.

In that, we are proud of our part in giving outstanding female athletes a place to thrive after their college careers ended. The WBA achieved God's vision. And to this day, I know that we fulfilled God's plan for all of us. ***If there hadn't been a WBA, there would not have been the WNBA.***

Lightning Ned Mitchell with Prime Sports at the All-Star Game

The Vision

Chapter 11
Postgame

Although I came to accept the abrupt termination of the WBA, something still gnawed at me. The way the league ended kept the players, coaches, managers, and owners from gaining the recognition they deserved. They had come together in purpose and willingly sacrificed their time and talents to be pioneers for the women's professional game. I set out on a new mission: to honor their contribution by ensuring they got the acknowledgment they were due.

I thought perhaps I could find someone to make a documentary about the league. As I searched the Internet trying to find a company that could help promote the story of the (WBA), I came across three or four companies in the Kansas City, Missouri, area and a few in Kansas. For some reason Laura Allen's company Allegra Media stood out among them all. I set up a meeting with her. After that conversation, I knew her company was the one for me. She took the WBA's story very seriously and wanted the world to know about it – especially every female athlete that loves the game of basketball. And as far as Laura was concerned, there was no greater moment than the WBA for women's sports since Title IX. She immediately stepped forward to see that the story was told, and she put me in a position to meet the right people. And she also became a partner with me in this whole venture.

She put me in touch with Cylk Cozart, an American actor who has played in more than thirty films and twenty television shows, including *Slam Dunk Ernest* and *White Men Can't Jump*. At the time he was already working on a basketball documentary called *Fast Break*. I phoned him at his home in Knoxville, Tennessee, and we talked about what I was trying to do.

"You need to come to Knoxville," he said. "We have the Women's Basketball Hall of Fame here. Your story needs to be in there."

I drove to Knoxville, and Cylk took me to see the Hall. The nonprofit international museum opened in 1999 and is dedicated to preserve the history of women's basketball at all levels. Its stated mission is to "Honor the Past, Celebrate the Present, and Promote the Future" of women's basketball.

We parked, and I was immediately impressed with the Hall's size and beauty – especially the world's largest basketball that sits on the roof. The thirty-foot diameter Báden basketball weights ten tons.

Cylk grinned. "What do you think?"

"It's spectacular," I said.

"Wait till you go inside."

The Vision

Inside, the Pat Summitt Rotunda was named for the University of Tennessee's women's basketball coach for thirty-eight years (1974-2012). Her teams made thirty-one consecutive NCAA tournament appearances and won eight national titles. She was the first basketball coach (men's or women's) to win 1,000 games.

The rotunda, with its wide staircase and wraparound balcony sported the seventeen-foot-high, bronze Eastman statue. Each inductee gets a smaller replica of the sculpture. The displays each had so much to look at you could easily spend ten to fifteen minutes viewing it. There were lists of women's basketball teams and features of outstanding players and coaches. Some displays included videos. I was so excited. There were so many exhibits, and I wanted to see them all. It was hard to decide which enticed me most. I got caught up in the moment. It was like a wonderful Christmas gift.

In addition to Pat Summitt's honors, I enjoyed seeing tributes to such coaches as Vivian Stringer from the University of Iowa and later Rutgers University, Marian Washington from the University of Kansas, and Leon Barmore from Louisiana Tech University. All of them had been instrumental in supporting the WBA. They did everything they could to help me get players to tryouts.

One exhibit features the stretch limousine used by the All American Red Heads, a professional women's basketball exhibition team that played for fifty years from 1936 to 1986. Seeing it reminded me of the rental vans the WBA traveled in on its exhibition tour. The

Hall also has an area called the Urban Playground. It depicts an urban basketball court, including a chain link fence, bleachers, and walls covered with graffiti.

As Cylk and I wandered through the Hall, I came upon a photo of Val Ackerman, the woman credited with starting the WNBA. Nearby was an exhibit of the American Basketball League. The ABL was an independent professional women's basketball league that played two season between 1996 and 1998. It went bankrupt and folded on December 22, 1998.

What are they doing in here? I wondered. The WBA played three entire seasons and there's no mention of us in the Hall. That's when I was sure I needed to work with diligence to get the league and players into the Hall and give them a place to take their children and grandchildren and say, "I was a part of that."

For the last twenty years their efforts have been unknown to the world. They had given everything to be pioneers of something great. I had to tell their story.

Now, dear readers, I ask for your help. Please contact the Women's Basketball Hall of Fame to show your support for including the WBA and its players in the Hall. Write to 700 Hall of Fame Drive, Knoxville, TN 37915. Or, call (865) 633-9000. You can also e-mail them through their website:

http://www.wbhof.com/Contact.html.

Please help me get these pioneers the recognition they deserve.

Where Are They Now?

Sarah Campbell

Sarah Campbell retired as an athlete from professional women's basketball, but she stayed in the game as a coach. She has coached in both the high school and college ranks and coached in the professional ranks for the Kansas Nuggets in the WBCBL. She now serves as general manager and co-owner of Kansas City Majestics Basketball." Basketball has always been a passion of mine since I was little," she said. "Having a Kansas City women's basketball team means I am able to give women an opportunity to continue to execute their talents on a higher level. This team allows me to use my talents and skills to give back to the community. Sarah's professional career has been in management, fifteen years with UPS and now operations manager at Lineage Logistics. She lives in Belton, Missouri with her family.

Dr. Robelyn "Robbie" Garcia

Dr. Robelyn "Robbie" Garcia is a multidisciplinary professor and Post-Doc Scholar at Personal Professors Academy and Arizona State University, where she is the recipient of the ASU College of Health Solutions Graduate Grant. Additionally, she teaches geriatric wellness, health, biogerontology, and kinesiology classes online and in person at Senior University in Scottsdale, Arizona.

Further, she is the president emeritus of her Jr. NBA-WNBA charter program, vice-president of American Community Team Sports, a Dodge City College Hall of Fame member, and founder of Dr. Robelyn Garcia Scholarships. She began offering scholarships in 2011 in honor of her late mother and launched her scholarship program in 2015. She continues to offer basketball scholarships for Jr. NBA-

WNBA camps in addition to sponsoring Seniors 50+, WBCBL teams and college scholar athletes. She is the official sponsor of the Senior University Wii Sports team, winner of state and conference National Senior League Championships. She is also very proud to be the official uniform sponsor of the new women's professional WBCBL Kansas City basketball team coached by two of her WBA teammates.

Professor Garcia has eight college degrees, including a PhD in Education, a master's of science degree in kinesiology and exercise science, a master's of education in passing, a graduate certificate in biogerontology, a master's in aging and lifespan development, an associate's, bachelor's, and master's of arts in criminal justice. She currently has a post-doc fellowship in the ASU Graduate Studies program and began her second doctoral program at ASU in 2014 with an anticipated conferral date in 2017-2018.

Supplementing her post-secondary degrees, research, and teaching, she has published several works, including her *Guide to Coaching Youth Basketball* and other academic papers. She holds a seat on the volunteer editorial board of *The International Journal of Complementary and Alternative Medicine.*

When Robbie is not busy working, she spends her time cycling, exercising, and volunteering. She volunteered as a doctoral mentor and with the ASU Doctor of Behavioral Health student forum team. She also volunteers through bicycle charities, senior sports organizations, bike patrol, and Special Olympics.

Through all of her activities, her mission is to educate and motivate. As seen through the support of local programs, her lifelong passion is basketball. Moreover, she is a vocal advocate of health and crime prevention via sport, recreation, physical activity, and wellness.

The Vision

Petra Jackson

Petra Jackson lives in Orange County, California. After the WBA she was the head coach for basketball programs at St. Louis Community College-Forest Park in Missouri and Shoreline Community College in Seattle, Washington. She turned both into winning programs. She also was an assistant coach at St. Louis University. She co-coaches her son's AAU team Two One Elite, manages his acting career, and works full-time.

Sheryl Schroefel

Sheryl Schroefel's true passion is kids, coaching, and playing basketball, volleyball, and softball. She officiates volleyball, basketball, and softball. She also teaches physical education and health, and coaches at Casper Classical Academy, a sixth through ninth grade middle school. She coaches from the beginning to the end of the school year without a break: eighth grade girls' volleyball and basketball, sixth and eighth grade boys' basketball, and track. Her school mascot is the Cougars. She finds it interesting that she played for the Oklahoma Cougars in the WBA and still has the same mascot. "I thoroughly enjoyed playing for Lightning, because of his passion to see that women were treated fairly and to give us an opportunity to play here in the United States. I am thankful for everything Lightning did for us," she said.

The Vision

Diana Vines

In 2007 Diana Vines started Dvynes Intervention, an organization of educators, innovators, and facilitators with a purpose. The group implements a learning and intervention module that stands apart from the rest.

The Dvynes Intervention team has seen first-hand the consequences of our youth getting lost in the educational system and has set out to change that through an innovative approach, which engages students and better supports educators in their growth. The organization has led the effort to change the educational experience of children, young adults, and educators. Diana knows that hard work plus determination equals success better than anyone. She learned through her own experience as an inner-city youth and teenage mother that if she wanted a different life, she would have to create it. Despite life's challenges, Diana excelled through hard work with the support of coaches, teachers, and family. As a college and WBA professional basketball player for years, she used her fierce determination to carry her to become an inductee of both the Illinois High School Basketball Hall of Fame and the DePaul Athletic Hall of Fame. Diana has rounded out her career by giving back through teaching and coaching both student and professional athletes. Her main focus is shaping the minds of young athletes by focusing on real-world, life-changing higher education to ensure success beyond the game. She earned a bachelor's degree in education from DePaul received recognition for twenty-five years of service in teaching. She also received a plaque for twenty-plus years of coaching in Natrona County School District. She earned a bachelor's degree in education from DePaul University and a master's degree in adult education and training from the University of Phoenix. She is working toward a PhD in curriculum instruction and design from Walden University.

Women's Blue-Chip Basketball League, LLC

In November 2004, Willie McCray founded the Women's Blue-Chip Basketball League as a developmental organization to aid female basketball athletes in their goals to become professional players through ministry and competitive play.

This league has two similarities to the WBA, and I'm happy to see how well their mission aligns with the WBA's. First, like the WBA, the WBCBL was founded by a man of faith who was pursuing a professional football career. Second, both leagues sought to offer ways for women to continue their basketball careers in the United States after the college experience.

I'm happy to say that former University of Missouri standout player Sarah Campbell, who won two MVP awards when she played for the Kansas City Mustangs in the WBA is part of this organization. She is co-owner of the Kansas City Majestics and serves as the team's head coach. I like to think that her involvement is part of the WBA's legacy.

— *Lightning Ned Mitchell*

Interview with Willie McCray, founder and president

1. How did the club come to be?

Basketball has always been my favorite sport. No matter where I traveled, I always sought an opportunity to play. In 1998, I moved to Dallas from Menifee, Arkansas, in hopes of pursuing my professional football career. Unfortunately, my football playing days were cut short in 2001 due to injuries. During that time, I was invited to play pick-up ball with a group of former college and professional players. The guys use to tell stories about their travel team tours to different places and college exhibition games. I had always been interested in joining a traveling team, but didn't have any connections. I had no idea how simple it would be to start a travel team. It was literally only a matter of getting a few guys together and contacting local colleges to schedule preseason games.

2. Why did you start it?

I've always had a passion for basketball but not much opportunity to play in the area where I grew up. During the summer, we didn't have any AAU teams or any other youth sports programs, so my generation was limited to playing in the evenings at the city park in our small, rural town. Once school started, there was an

The Vision

inner frustration of seeing other kids get all of the attention, while my homies and I rode the bench as victims of the "Ol buddy-buddy" system. (The kids whose parents were friends of the coaches got far more than their fair-share of playing-time.) We knew we were just as talented and athletic as our peers, but didn't get a fair chance to show it.

The injustice and favoritism created a long-lasting memory and drive to prove that I was better than they assumed and that everyone deserves a chance to shine. Upon my various playing experiences in the Dallas area, I met many others that fell in the same "box" as me and my friends. It didn't take much time for me to decide that I would try to help as many as I could to get that chance to prove what they could do on the court.

3. What are the advantages and disadvantages of starting the club?

The advantages of starting the Dallas Diesel was instant name recognition associated with

"Opportunity" and "A Good Thing." Our slogan, "Giving Opportunity to the Community" sent a positive vibe throughout DFW and offered hope to those seeking to fulfill a once prior denied dream. Our Mission Statement reads, "The mission of Dallas Diesel Basketball Club, Inc. (DDBC) is to develop athletes and build social character within local communities. DDBC provides an opportunity for its members to reach their personal goals through ministry and athletic competition." The disadvantages have been mainly related to lack of working capital and minimal funding from an occasional sponsor. There is so much potential for our organization, but we have to have money to cover the expense of success.

4. What are the strengths and weaknesses of the club?

The strength of the Dallas Diesel is our Christian foundation, which by faith, has carried us through thirteen years of operating successfully. Second, our members are unique and come from various walks of life. This combination mixed with a restless pursuit of determination and focus has us on track to achieve a consistency of excellence. The weakness of the club lies within the amount of time spent on key tasks, such as fundraising and engaging in city chamber of commerce events. All of our members have busy lives: families, fulltime jobs and some are also taking classes.

5. How did the club help build the WBCBL?

The birth of the WBCBL (Women's Blue Chip Basketball League, LLC) came from the fast growing popularity of the Dallas Diesel Women's program sending players overseas to play professionally. For years, we sought a minor league for our Dallas Diesel women's team, but there were not any within the Southwest region of the United States.

After hosting a series of open tryouts, we had a gym full of very talented players who came from the East Coast, West Coast, and even Japan and London (UK)! I

The Vision

was like, "Wow, are there not any teams in your states?" Their answers were "No, that's why we're here." At that point, it was clear that we would have to start our own league to accommodate such a large void that demanded to be filled, and the WBCBL was born.

6. What is the WBCBL?

In November 2004, Willie McCray founded the Women's Blue-Chip Basketball League as a developmental organization to aid female basketball athletes in their goals to become professional players through ministry and competitive play. The WBCBL provides players with top rate competition, exposure to pro scouts, and spiritual mentorship. The league has grown to have teams in twenty-three states and totaling more than thirty-five teams nationwide in North America.

7. What would you like to improve in any aspect of the club?

My main concern for each of our club teams is to remember their roots and to continue building upon our Christian foundation and principles. I would like to get churches involved with each team to strength the spiritual aspect. Besides that, our brand recognition and our community relations can definitely use a big booster shot. I believe this area would create a domino effect and lead to us acquiring some much needed sponsors.

8. Where do you see the club going in the future?

My vision for the Dallas Diesel is to become the household name for athletics and secondary education in North Texas. To become an institution with a campus and provide housing, career training, and refuge for those in need of our assistance.

9. Where do you see the WBCBL going in the future?

I definitely see the WBCBL becoming the premier league for women's basketball throughout North America and a few foreign countries. The WBCBL has a steady growth rate and features some of the best talent in the world, that's not in the WNBA. Since our start, the WBCBL has featured former WNBA players and professional international players.

10. What was your greatest achievement from starting this club?

My single greatest achievement from starting the Dallas Diesel Basketball Club, was for a young man to be led to Christ by the living testimonies and the care shown through our efforts to help people. He went from being a hustler in the streets to a ranking military officer and married with his own family. We lost touch after his first season with us. However, ten years later, he called to thank me for everything we did to help him get on the right path.

Romans 10:9

"That if you confess with your mouth, "Jesus is Lord," and believe in your heart that God raised Him from the dead, you will be saved."

Women's Blue-Chip
Basketball League, LLC
www.WBCBL.com
P.O. Box 1622
Rowlett, TX 75030
Ph: 214-810-7406
Fax: 1+ 877-810-7406

WBA Timeline

1991

- Lightning Mitchell answers God's call to found and direct a professional women's basketball league.

1992

- Lightning Mitchell contacts NCAA Divsions I, II, and III women's basketball coaches for assistance promoting the league and finding interested players.
- Lightning Mitchell resists God's call. He sets up tests and obstacles to make God prove Himself.
- The WBA holds tryouts at the Milwaukee Bucks training facility, a wing of the Archbishop Cousins Center in St. Francis, Wisconsin.
- The Women's World Basketball Association (WWBA) goes on an eight-city exhibition tour.

1993

- Lightning Mitchell takes a job at Kraft Tool in Kansas City, Missouri. His boss tells him to devote one hundred and ten percent of his time to the basketball league.
- *Women's Sports and Fitness* publishes article about the league
- League's official name changed to the Women's

Basketball Association (WBA).
- League sets up franchises in six cities: Beatrice, Nebraska; Cedar Rapids, Iowa; Kansas City, Kansas; Kansas City, Missouri; Quincy, Illinois; Tulsa, Oklahoma.
- Season begins April 10.
- The Kansas Crusaders beat the Nebraska Xpress 100-96 to win the first-ever WBA Championship game.

1994

- Lightning Mitchell seeks sponsorships for the WBA from Michael Jordan, Magic Johnson, and the NBA.
- Lightning Mitchell sells two franchises: The Kansas City Mustangs and the St. Louis RiverQueens.
- Kansas Crusaders change name to Kansas Marauders.
- Oklahoma Cougars move to Tulsa, Oklahoma, and change name to Oklahoma Flames.
- The Illinois Knights move to Gary, Indiana, as the Indiana Stars expansion team.
- The Iowa Unicorns remain in Cedar Rapids, and change name to the Iowa Twisters.
- Expansion team also forms as the Memphis Blues in Tennessee.
- All teams get new logos.
- Nebraska Xpress wins the 1994 Championship Game.

1995

The Vision

- Chicago Twisters and Minnesota Stars franchises form.
- Kandi Conda makes a deposit to buy the Twisters.
- Iowa Twisters and Indiana Stars fold in favor of franchises in bigger markets.
- Liberty Sports buys six teams in the WBA and agrees to broadcast games.
- WBA All-Star Game in Kansas City, Missouri, attracts 3,426 fans. National Conference wins 89-67.
- Chicago Twisters beat the St. Louis RiverQueens to take the crown in the 1995 WBA championship game.

1996

- American Basketball League announces plans to form a women's professional basketball leagues. Promises average player salaries of $70,000.
- Liberty Sports wants to buy two remaining franchises.
- Kansas City Mustangs owners sell, but the St. Louis RiverQueens and Liberty sports fail to come to terms.
- Liberty Sports walks away.
- WBA folds.

2008

- Lightning Mitchell sets out to get recognition for the WBA and its players.
- During research about the league, Lightning Mitchell discovers that Val Ackerman was the founder of the WNBA.

- Lightning Mitchell sues the NBA and WNBA for $500 million for mental distress.
- Case is time barred and dismissed due to expiration of the statute of limitations.
- Lightning Mitchell continues to seek recognition of the WBA and its players.

Photos of WBA Players and Teams

WBA player Evette Ott shown here as a professional business woman during the week and a pro basketball player on the weekend

Robelyn Garcia of the Kansas Crusaders 1993

Oklahoma Cougars team of 1993

Nebraska Xpress player Sandy Skradski signing autographs for fans

WBA American Conference All-Star players of 1994

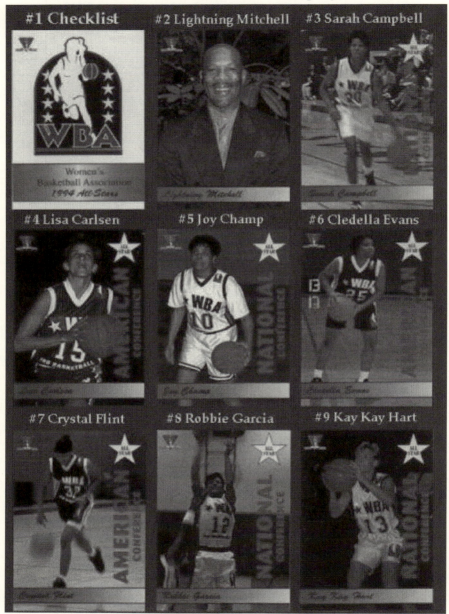

WBA trading cards of 1994

Becky Inman-Han, left, drives toward the basket against Oklahoma's Lynn Pape. Inman-Han, a Chesterton graduate, scored 15 points for Indiana

Indiana Stars home game with
Oklahoma Flames

Chicago Twisters's Diana Vines making a break for a layup during a playoff game with St. Louis RiverQueens at their home court

The Vision

Kansas City Mustangs team of 1995

Lightning Ned Mitchell and Sarah Campbell

Newspaper Articles

SPORTS

KANSAS CITY KANSAN, Tuesday, Aug. 10, 1993   7

Crusaders smell crown

By MARK LEE
Kansan Sports Writer

The Kansas Crusaders are just one win away from claiming the Women's Basketball Association championship.

Kansas, which played its regular season games at Eisenhower Recreation Center, can wrap up the title Wednesday night. The Crusaders and Nebraska play Game 4 of their best-of-5 series at Penn Valley Community College (7:30). Kansas leads the series 2-1 following a 111-96 win Saturday night over the Express.

"It feels good," Kansas coach Jamie Collins said. "Our victory Saturday night took a lot of the pressure off of us. Now the pressure is on Nebraska. They have to win or the series is over. It would be great to win it before our fans."

If Kansas loses Wednesday, the fifth and deciding game would be played in Beatrice, Neb., on Saturday. Collins said it is important to win the title at home.

"Everybody is extremely excited, especially from the standpoint that we want to try to do it at home," Collins said. "It would be really sweet to finish it out at home in front of our fans who have followed us since April."

Collins said her game plan won't change any for Wednesday's game. She feels her Crusaders will be charged up.

"We've got to play four quarters of basketball," Collins said. "After 22 games this season, it's not going to change at all. It's whoever wants it the most. We just have to execute and be more emotionally ready."

Defense has been the key all season long for the Crusaders, who held the hot-shooting Express to just 96 points Saturday. That's the first time the Express have scored under 100 points against Kansas in six games this season.

"It was a combination of great second half defense and poor shooting by Nebraska," Collins said. "We just cranked it up on defense. They weren't hitting their shots and I credit that to our defense."

Evette Ott led Kansas with 24 points Saturday before injuring her ankle in the fourth quarter. Ott's status is uncertain for Wednesday's game.

"She was walking on it and that's always a good sign," Collins said. "She will go in for treatment and won't do anything until Wednesday at the game. She came down on somebody's foot while getting a rebound. She has a pretty good sprained ankle. Those usually hurt the worst.

"It will be a day-to-day thing right now. It will take horses to keep her back. She's too much of a competitor."

Four other Kansas players scored in double figures Saturday.

Kansas Crusaders hope to keep the clamps on Nebraska just his Crusader player is doing at the right.

C-10 The Kansas City Star Sunday, May 28, 1995 ★ ★ ★

National All-Stars run past Americans in WBA game

By BILL RICHARDSON
Staff Writer

Speed and defense made the difference as the National Conference rallied for an 89-67 victory over the American Conference in the Women's Basketball Association All-Star Game Saturday night at Municipal Auditorium.

The Nationals, trailing after three quarters, rallied in the fourth quarter and outscored the Americans 36-8 in front of an announced crowd of 3,426, the largest in the three-year history of the host Kansas City Mustangs.

Forward Ronda Lauderdale of Memphis and guard Laurie Byrd of Kentucky paced the Nationals. Lauderdale made successive three-point baskets and pulled the Nationals ahead 63-61. She finished with a game-high 18 points. She also won the award for most valuable player. Byrd finished with 15 points, and Danielle Shareef of St. Louis, who played at Kansas, had 11.

Byrd capped the fourth-quarter surge with four straight baskets as the torrid fast break of the Nationals wore down their opponents.

"The coach told us to get in and run and have fun," Byrd said. "She put in our fast squad, and we ran the break real well. We were the home team, and the crowd got into the game, and that helped."

National Coach Jean Pate of St. Louis said the turnaround was a matter of timing.

"I was trying to get everybody 6 minutes a quarter, and the timing rotation worked out just right," Pate said. "But the way we were going, I wasn't going to change back with the speed and quickness we had going."

Renee Dozier of Nebraska led the American squad with 13 points. Jo Mosley of Oklahoma added 12 points. But the Americans went cold in the fourth quarter.

"At one point there, we missed 11 shots in a row," American Coach Stephanie Tamayo-Rivera of Chicago said.

JEREL HARRIS/Special to The Star
The Kansas City Mustangs' Lisa Tate brought down a rebound Saturday during the WBA All-Star Game.

RiverQueens Lose In WBA Title Game

By Jeremy Rutherford
Special to the Post-Dispatch

The RiverQueens fared well against most of their Women's Basketball Association foes this season, but just couldn't beat the Chicago Twisters. And that was the case again Saturday night, in the league's title contest.

Chicago took an early lead and rolled to a 107-96 victory before a crowd of about 1,000 at the University of Missouri-St. Louis.

The 'Queens were 9-6 in the regular season, with two of the losses coming to the Twisters, who were 14-1.

The RiverQueens had one last chance Saturday, after Petra Jackson made six free throws as Chicago was assessed three technical fouls in slightly more than a minute. The barrage cut their deficit to 97-91 with 2 minutes 28 seconds remaining.

But the Twisters had an answer for every RiverQueens basket in the final minutes.

"They scored every time that we didn't need them to," said Jackson, who had a game-high 32 points. "They came through in the clutch, and that happens."

Saturday was supposed to be the night the RiverQueens opened the second round of the WBA playoffs. But last week the league decided to cancel its six-team playoff system to preserve funds for next season.

Because Chicago and the 'Queens had each won their respective conferences, the league staged a one-game championship.

Jackson scored six points, giving the RiverQueens an early 10-7 lead. But the Twisters tied the game 12-12 and opened a 22-17 lead after the first quarter.

"We were prepared for their adjustments," Chicago coach Stephanie Rivera said. "Even though we were prepared, we made some mistakes. But we stayed calm and got back into our offense."

The Twisters held a 43-34 halftime advantage, and had a little help from the RiverQueens — they had 15 first-half turnovers.

Coach Jean Pate said: "We only had a couple of more turnovers than they did, but ours were caused more by not running our offense."

As a result, the Twisters increased their lead to 17 points (58-41) midway through the third quarter. But the

Jerry Naunheim Jr./Post-Dispatch
Chicago's Natalie Perrino (left) tries to find a way around the RiverQueens' Nikki Anderson in Saturday night's title game at UMSL.

RiverQueens, who played with only four substitutes, kept nipping away.

"We weren't going to give up," Pate said. "But we couldn't get the ball to fall for us. Every time we cut the lead to six points, they'd run away again. Chicago has equal scoring all the way down their bench."

Nine Twisters scored, led by Diana Vines' 31 points.

Danielle Shareef had 24 points for the RiverQueens and was followed by Sarita Wesley with 16 and Renee Bishop with 10.

The Vision

PRO BASKETBALL: Three members of the Nebraska Express team who have area ties are, from left, Shannon Struby, former Millard South and Creighton University player; Maurtice Ivy, former Omaha Central and Nebraska player; and Kelly Luenenborg, Millard South graduate who played for the University of Nebraska at Kearney.

No Pay for These Pros
Nebraska Team Wants Women's League to Survive

BY ROB WHITE
WORLD-HERALD STAFF WRITER

Members of the Nebraska Express women's professional basketball team are playing for the competition and not for the money.

There isn't any money.

"Since we don't get a lot of fan support, it's difficult for them to pay us to play," forward Renee Dozier said. "Hopefully in the future that's something that will happen."

The Express won the Women's Basketball Association's American Conference with a 10-5 regular-season record and earned a first-round bye in the playoffs.

Nebraska will play host to the Indiana Stars at 7:30 p.m. Saturday and 1:30 p.m. Sunday in the best-of-three American Conference championship series at Omaha Benson. If a third game is needed, it would be played July 22 at Indiana or at Kansas City if that franchise wins the Nation-

Please turn to Page 29, Col. 1

Women's Professional Basketball Leagues Built on Faith

The Vision

Resources for Girls' and Women's Basketball

Amateur Athletic Union (AAU)
AAU National Headquarters
PO Box 22409
Lake Buena Vista, FL 32830

Boys and Girls Clubs of America
National Headquarters
1275 Peachtree Street NE
Atlanta, GA 30309-3506

Fellowship of Christian Athletes
FCA National Support Center
8701 Leeds Road
Kansas City, MO 64129

International Basketball Federation (FIBA)
Route Suisse 5 - P.O Box 29
1295 Mies – Switzerland

National Association of Intercollegiate Athletes (NAIA)

1200 Grand Blvd.
Kansas City, MO 64106

National Catholic Youth Organization
415 Michigan Ave NE, STE 40
Washington, DC 20017

The National Collegiate Athletic Association (NCAA)
700 W. Washington Street
P.O. Box 6222
Indianapolis, Indiana 46206-6222

United States Basketball Association
2275 Captain Waring Ct.
Mt. Pleasant, South Carolina 29466

Women's National Basketball Association (WNBA)
Olympic Tower, 645 Fifth Avenue
New York, NY 10022

YMCA of the USA
101 N Wacker Drive
Chicago, IL 60606

Youth Basketball of America (YBOA)
YBOA
7676 Municipal Drive
Orlando, FL 32819

Assists (Acknowledgments)

Many thanks to all the players, coaches, managers, and staff of the WBA.

Also to the following people, who encouraged me, Bob Hawkins, Joann Johnson, Sandra Kay Mitchell, Joe Lee Mitchell, Willie and Alyce Mitchell, Linda Mae (Mitchell-Bell) Flowers, Glenda V. Mitchell, Derk Mitchell, Chubby Mitchell, Ann Smith, Debbie Summers, Pee Wee Summers, and Kandi Conda.

Also to the college coaches who helped me make connections, and sent players to tryouts. Leon Barmore, Louisiana Tech University; Marcus Harvey, Penn Valley Community College; Vivian Stringer, University of Iowa; Pat Summitt, University of Tennessee; Marian Washington, University of Kansas.

Finally, appreciation goes to the many businesses that supported the WBA with trade-outs for meals, hotel rooms, T-shirts, printing, door prizes, and championship trophies and rings. Athletes in Action, Baker's

Square, Budget Inn, Burger King, Comfort Inn, Days Inn, Denny's, Econo Lodge, Enterprise Leasing, Hardee's, Fair Play, Fellowship of Christian Athletes, Josten Jewelry, KC Screen Print, Kentucky Fried Chicken, Liberty Sports, McDonald's, Motel 6, Sir Speedy Print, Ramada Inn, Red Roof Inn, Russell Sports, Saxes Sporting Goods, Super 8, and *Women's Sports and Fitness* magazine, as well as local restaurants who sponsored the WBA.

My Prayer

I hope you enjoyed reading this book and seeing how the Lord worked through my life. God has a plan for all of us in some way, shape, or form. All we need to do is to believe and trust Him to see us through with it. And by the way, if you haven't accepted Him already, I invite you to do so now.

It's simple. For example: Just pray, Lord, I know you're the son of God, who died for a sinner like me. I'm asking you to forgive me for my sins, and I accept you, Jesus, as my Lord and Savior. And I'm asking You to help me to be the person you created me to be for your kingdom and glory. Amen.

I told you it was simple. Now just believe it, and Jesus will do the rest.

Always God bless,
Lightning Mitchell

Now You Know the True Story

Index

A

Abrahamson, Katie, 57
Ackerman, Valerie, 71, 129, 132, 150
Aldridge, Chris, 25, 78, 79, 87, 93, 94, 113, 119
Amole, Brett, 34
Arnold, Christa, 85

B

Bacon, Jean, 84, 85
Bakhaus, Lori, 106
Ballenger, Denise, 84, 92
Barmore, Leon, 14, 161
Bayh, Birch, 1
Becker, Robin, 56, 64, 84, 85, 92, 94
Bell, Ketra, 112
Benson, Brook, 69, 87
Bishop, Renee, 78, 113, 123

Blair, Carolyn, 81, 89, 93, 109, 119
Blunk, Krista, 108
Braddy, Lisa, 59, 68, 79, 107, 119
Bragg, Robin, 57
Brooks, Keesha, 85
Brown, Shawna, 107
Brown-Glascoe, Tatya, 112
Burch, Lisa, 26, 35, 36
Burer, Tom, 19
Bye, Dale, 61
Byrd, Laurie, 118, 119

C

Campbell, Sarah, 51, 63, 64, 69, 75, 86, 87, 93, 94, 107, 121, 139, 169
Carlsen, Lisa, 28, 111, 120
Carney, Staci, 97, 105, 106
Carr, Sharon, 82
Catchings, Harvey, 97

Champ, Joy, 68, 75, 79, 107, 121
Clark, Michelle, 108
Clemons, Toinetta, 78, 80
Coates, Nicole, 33
Cobb, Arneetrice, 85, 93
Coffman, Andrea, 78, 80
Coffman, Dale, 78
Cole, Annette, 85
Collins, Jamie, 47, 65, 67, 68, 69, 105, 107, 112, 116
Conda, Kandi, 96, 97, 104, 106, 114, 124, 127, 128, 149, 161
Conner, Cindy, 97
Covington, Audrey, 109
Cox, Pam, 27
Crawford, Sarina, 109
Cummings, Dewart, 98

D

Dale, Julie, 61, 78, 111
Davis, Lori, 109, 120
Davis, Tracye, 108
Deeken, Dee Dee, 110, 120
Donald, Terri, 89, 90, 109, 119, 120
Dougherty, Kelly, 33
Dozier, Renee, 27, 60, 66, 69, 88, 92, 94, 111, 118, 120
Dudley, Carla, 92

Duncan, Marla, 112
Dunn, Judy, 103

E

Edges-Ward, Patty Jo, 119
Edwards, Colleen, 85, 93
Eichorst, Angie, 85
Ereiser, Janet, 66
Ervin, Latarice, 107
Evans, Cledella, 112

F

Faber, Mark, 103
Fields, Larry, 31, 56, 60, 64, 84, 85, 92
Fisher, Kamiel, 85
Fitzgerald, James, 8
Flint, Crystal, 110
Flowers, Linda Mae (Mitchell-Bell), 161
Foli, Diane, 60, 69
Folkl, Kristin, 78
Fordham, Amy, 121
Fowler, LaRon, 112

G

Galindo, Nadine, 106
Ganahl, Julie, 57
Gant, Lashon, 107
Garcia, Robelyn Annette, 26, 39, 59, 68, 69, 78,

79, 116, 118, 126, 137, 152
Garrett, Helen, 86, 92, 112, 120
Garvin, Margo, 76, 127
Garvin, Paul, 113
Gary, Priscilla, 15, 25, 41, 42, 81, 109, 148
Geick, Lynn, 100, 101, 103, 127
Gittens, Dawne, 36
Gritts, Larissa, 112

H

Hadley, Stephanie, 112
Hanks, Bill, 78, 93, 113
Harris, CeCi, 75
Harris, Terrance, 61
Hart, Geri, 26, 104
Harter, Mike, 103
Hartley, Kim, 108
Hawkins, Bob, 19, 23, 161
Hebert, Ellen, 110
Heddow, Lynn, 99
Hedges-Ward, Patty Jo, 108
Hermann, Karen, 78
Hester, Chris, 110
Hill, Denise, 108
Hill, E.C., 97, 105, 106, 129
Hilton, Bob, 57
Hippen, Melinda, 85

Hogan, Lori, 84, 85
Holahan, Maureen, 97, 106
Holston, Patrick, 89
Horn, Dixie, 92
Hough, Carla, 64
Hovet, Tiny, 31, 41, 54, 55
Howard, Sarah, 110

I

Inman-Han, Becky, 81
Ivey, Niele, 78
Ivy, Maurtice, 51, 59, 60, 62, 67, 69, 86, 88, 90, 92, 94, 111

J

Jackson, Petra, 79, 80, 93, 94, 113, 116, 119, 122, 123, 124, 128
Jackson, Teresa, 78, 80
Jacobs, Monica, 76
Jennings, Karen, 60, 66
Johnson, Gina, 85
Johnson, Magic, 60, 71, 148
Johnson, Terrilyn, 66, 68, 81, 92, 94
Jones, Jennifer, 82, 105, 106
Jones, Stephanie, 121
Jones, Wanda, 90, 109

Jordan, Michael, 27, 60, 71, 96, 148

K

Kee, Lorraine, 77
Kenkel, Lisa, 69
Kirby, Lisa, 112
Klotzbeecher, Mary, 110
Kriewall, Randy, 78, 113
Kundinger, Stacy, 105, 106

L

Lauderdale, Ronda, 109, 118, 119, 120
Lewis, Angie, 78
Lieberman, Nancy, 14, 119
Long, Lisa, 25, 59, 60, 64, 84, 85, 86, 92, 94, 112
Long, Scott, 111
Luenenborg, Kelly, 88

M

Manual, Chris, 99
Maravich,, 76
Marshall, Patrice, 112
Marte, Andrea, 121
Maurstad, Dave, 54
McCallister, Fred D., 101, 103
McClelland, Kim, 113
McCray, Willie, 139, 141, 144
McDonnagh, Nora, 82
McFarlan, Rose, 85
McFarquhar, Angela (Mitchell), 131
McKinzie, Mark, 92
Meriweather, Joe C., 46, 48, 75, 87, 105, 107
Messer, Sid, 54
Meyer, Ron, 44
Miller, Erica, 68
Mitchell, Alyce, 32, 161
Mitchell, Joe Lee, 3, 29, 98, 161
Mitchell, Sandra, 131, 169
Mitchell, Willie, 9, 41
Mitts, Maryann, 68
Mobely, Kathy, 110
Morgan, Joe Jr., 107
Morton, Willie, 35
Mosley, Jo, 112, 120

N

Nichols, Leslie, 108
Niehaus, Jan, 110, 120
Nixon, Richard, 1

O

Oberbeck, Angie, 85

Ott, Evette, 62, 66, 67, 68, 69, 75, 79, 80, 93, 94, 107, 119, 121, 163

P

Pack, Cassandra, 82
Page, Lynn, 26, 86, 92, 112, 120
Pate, Jean, 118, 123
Perrino, Natalie, 97, 105, 106
Potter, Jim, 54
Price, Joyce, 108
Prince, Alesia, 66, 68
Pryor, Beverly, 109

Q

Queen, Tony, 110

R

Randall, Harvey, 105
Rasheed, Tynetta, 111
Redwine, Paul, 56
Reiser, Janet, 60
Rivera, Ron, 97
Robinson, Lea, 108
Rohlfing, Kim, 78, 80
Rose, Jim, 97
Rutter, Veronica, 110

S

Sandbothe, Lisa, 78, 113
Sanford, Melissa, 27, 60, 69, 111, 120
Saxer, John, 19
Scaife, Pamela, 109
Schafer, Janet, 35, 36
Schmidt, Vickie, 14
Schroefel, Sheryl, 28, 40
Schueler, Steph, 57
Scott, Leatrice, 108, 111
Shareef, Danielle, 63, 75, 93, 119, 123
Shelton, Chris, 78
Skalicky, Kelly, 110
Skradski, Sandy, 60, 66, 69, 92, 94, 165
Smith Crystal, 109
Smith, Ann, 19, 23, 161
Smith, Charmin, 78, 128
Steelandt, Kim, 85
Steffen, Joan, 57
Stephens, Dawn, 85
Sterling, Jodi, 85
Stern, David, 71, 132
Stringer, Vivian, 14, 161
Struby, Shannon, 88, 111
Summers Pee Wee, 47, 102, 161
Summers, Debbie, 101, 105, 161
Summitt, Pat, 14, 161

Sun Electric, 8, 28, 32
Sweeney Priscilla, 81, 93, 109, 121
Sweet, Nova, 108

T

Tadich, Molly, 110, 120
Tamayo-Rivera, Stephanie, 97, 105, 106, 118, 122
Taplin, Annie, 93
Tate, Lisa, 107, 119, 121
Taylor, Lana, 82
Taylor, Rissa, 111
Thomas, Lashawne, 107, 121
Thompson, Bolivia, 106
Thompson, Calvin, 105, 121
Truitt, Stacy, 64, 66, 68, 75, 79, 93, 94, 121
Tunley, Yvett, 66, 68
Tunsil, Nicole, 92
Turnipseed, Connie, 46

U

Ulsaker, Melissa, 107

V

Veerhusen, Trudi, 69
Viergutz, Bruce M., 54

Vines, Diana, 24, 64, 81, 86, 92, 94, 97, 105, 106, 120, 123, 124, 137, 168

W

Wahsgton, Acquaneha, 106
Walker, Ann, 80, 85, 113
Ward, Angiline, 120
Washington, Marian, 14, 125, 161
Weise, Bob, 78
Welenc, Sue, 82
Wellman, Susan, 78, 80, 93, 113
Wesley, Sarita, 123
Westmoreland, Renee, 108
White, Jane, 56
White, Willye, 97
Williams, Tammy, 97, 106, 120
Williamson, Trish, 25, 34, 35, 36
Wilson, Mike, 9
Wilson, Queen, 110
Woodard, Lynnette, 14
Worthy, Stephanie, 26, 75, 76, 79, 93, 94, 107
Wyatt, Noel, 85

Y

Yedjena, Meggan, 111

The Vision

About the Authors

Lightning Mitchell was the founder and president of the Women's Basketball Association from 1991 to 1995. He was born in Hodge, Louisiana, and graduated from Jackson High School in Jonesboro, Louisiana. After two years in the U.S. Army, he returned to Hodge with plans to go back to college and eventually play professional football. He attended William Jewell College in Liberty, Missouri, and Arizona State University in Tempe, Arizona. He later played minor league football and attended NFL tryouts with the Philadelphia Eagles and Green Bay Packers. He worked at several other jobs before obeying God's call to start a women's professional basketball league. He lives in Independence, Missouri, with his wife Sandra Mitchell.

Mary-Lane Kamberg is an award-winning professional writer, speaker, and former basketball mom. She is the author of *North Carolina Basketball* (Rosen Publishing, 2013), as well as more than twenty-five other books and hundreds of magazine and newspaper articles, many on sports and health and fitness topics. She has a bachelor's of science degree in journalism from the University of Kansas and cheers for the Jayhawks during March Madness. She lives in Olathe, Kansas, with her husband, Ken Kamberg.

Made in the USA
Columbia, SC
22 May 2019